RT HON HENRY MCLEISH began
government in 1974, and
1987 he was elected as a member of the UK Parl
Devolution and Home Affairs in the Labour Gove
first Scottish Parliament he was Minister for Enter
1999, and in 2000 he became First Minister of Sc
politics in 2003, he is now an adviser, consultant, writer, author and broadcaster
and   s in the USA and elsewhere on the European Union and politics. He
           Scottish Prisons Commission, which produced a report into sentencing
a   inal justice system entitled 'Scotland's Choice'. In 2010 he conducted a
ma   on the state of football in Scotland, which had been commissioned by
the   ootball Association, and chaired a commission into sport requested by
the Sco.   vernment. He is now an honorary professor at Edinburgh University.

Citizens United

Taking Back Control in Turbulent Times

HENRY McLEISH

Luath Press Limited

EDINBURGH

www.luath.co.uk

First published 2017

ISBN: 978-1-910021-78-1

The paper used in this book is recyclable. It is made from low chlorine pulps
produced in a low energy, low emission manner from renewable forests.

Printed and bound by
Martins the Printers, Berwick upon Tweed

Typeset in 11 point Sabon by Main Point Books, Edinburgh

Contents

Preface

Citizens United: Taking Back Control in Turbulent Times was inspired by five concerns. First, a lifetime commitment to the enduring principles of the Labour party, whose fortunes have dipped in recent times. Second, a fear that our politics, democracy and governance were at risk, with darker forces trying to supplant progressive politics with populism, a market philosophy and a drift to the right. Third, the state of a declining Britain and the consequences for Scotland and the other nations as England starts to stir awkwardly from its slumber. Fourth, the idea that people don't matter too much in our politics, apart from being asked to vote every few years; that they are lauded as consumers but rarely recognised as citizens, a much more noble status. Fifth, more dramatically and worryingly, the momentous political year of 2016, the election of Trump in the US and the calamitous Brexit decision in the UK.

Trump and Brexit make no sense. It was like experiencing two bereavements where the cycle of grief kicks in and recovery is hindered by obsessing over the question: How did this happen?

This book's preparation was informed by numerous discussions with friends and colleagues in the US – in Denver, Tulsa, San Antonio, Tampa, New York and Washington, DC – as well as in London and Edinburgh.

Brexit stands out because of the direct threat it poses to Britain but also because of the remarkable step back in time delivered by the poisonous and reckless Leave campaign, celebrated by some as progress. For me, Brexit was a wake-up call.

The achievements of progressive politics were at risk.

Our politics need a radical transformation. There was nothing inevitable about the Trump-Brexit political shocks, but there is an urgency required in rethinking where we are as democrats, socialists and liberals in a world of social change, political upheaval, massive inequality and the cult of the 'tough guy' personality.

This book argues that this political upheaval is not just an unforeseen bump in the road; Trump and Brexit are earthquakes whose tremors are being felt throughout western democracies. Our guiding spirit in all of this must be the fact that both Trump and Brexit are consequences of something, not causes, and that is why the idea of drilling deeper and finding a new role for the citizen becomes so important: 63 million people voted for Trump and 17.4 million people voted for Brexit. These are big numbers, whose importance cannot be wished away.

Citizens United: Taking Back Control in Turbulent Times, is a warning about the need for change and an invitation to join the debate about what happens next. We must remain optimistic about the ability of humans to evolve and adapt. This book asks: How do we develop a more inspired politics where the citizen is valued and taken seriously?

Introduction

BRITAIN'S VOTE TO leave the European Union and the election of President Trump have sent shock waves through the democracies of Western Europe and have emboldened far right parties in Germany, France, Austria and the Netherlands. However, both France and the Netherlands have rejected far right politics with their respective elections of Emanuel Macron and Mark Rutte.

The striking and worrying similarities between the Trump and Brexit campaigns are a chilling reminder of how old ideas are being repackaged for modern times. History tells us about nationalism, however economic it is dressed up to be – authoritarianism, nativism, racism, xenophobia and religious intolerance (especially in the form of Islam) – and the consequences for countries and continents.

The political and press frenzy over Prime Minister Theresa May's future has tended to distract from the reality that a significant section of the Conservative party has embraced a cheap patriotism that is the enemy of what a modern Britain should be striving for. Personalities may change, but the right of the Conservative party doesn't. We ignore this basic fact at our peril.

Brexit is about the identity crisis that Britain has grappled with for over 70 years, and the question of Britain's role in the modern world, or the lack of one. It is about the failure of the right of the Conservative party and the UK Independence Party (UKIP) leadership to remove the shackles of the past and put behind them the nostalgia, sentiment and delusional mindset that refuses to accept that Britain no longer rules the waves or controls an empire and does not have a 'special' relationship with the United States – while also failing to see the significance continental Europe has for Britain in the 21st century.

The story on offer for Brexit, and for Trump, argues that all our ills are the fault of migrants, refugees, Muslims and Eastern European benefits tourists, who are simultaneously stealing all our jobs. In Britain, the story is further adorned by a barely concealed hostility to foreigners, especially the French and Germans, the supposed ringleaders in the EU's drive towards a federal state.

The story is rounded off with a generous helping of insidious nationalism (mainly English), a dash of isolationism and a hint of racism to come if Brexit succeeds.

These cheap patriots leading Brexit are consumed with a misplaced sense of history and are diminishing Britain in the eyes of the world.

Much of the developed world is experiencing political upheaval and in some cases radical political change. While there may be little agreement on where this is heading, there is compelling evidence about some of the causes: a deep disillusionment and anger with traditional politics; electorates freed from the patterns of previous voting; and growing anxieties about the inability of politicians and political parties to tackle the problems and challenges of our changing world. In this fragile anti-austerity environment, new parties are emerging and minority parties are gaining strength and enjoying varying degrees of success and popularity.

These are the politics of a turbulent, disgruntled and restless world. The EU, one of the most important political projects in history, faces threats, such as terrorism, migrants and narrow nationalism, that are reshaping the narrative.

We live in troubled times. In the wake of a remarkable political year, the winds of political change sweeping through western democracies have intensified, gaining momentum in 2017 and posing new challenges to the politics of social democracy and international solidarity.

Political certainties are being shredded with no end in sight.

It is of deep concern that 63 million people voted for Trump and 17.4 million people voted for Brexit. Trump's victory, exploiting Rust Belt resentment and racism in the US, is of crucial political significance: his authoritarianism threatens to destabilise the world order.

President Trump's tweets his support of the break-up of the EU, a view shared by Marie Le Pen of the National Front (who lost the election in France), the Alt-Right party in Germany and the far right Geert Wilders heading up NEXIT in the Netherlands (who also lost the election). Does Theresa May want to encourage the extremes of Europe's political right alongside Trump, and embrace them as new political allies? This is the 'new' populism of the right.

The EU referendum campaign was a sad but spectacular reminder of the fragile, volatile and uncertain nature of our democracy and politics.

The shallowness of our democracy has been laid bare. This campaign was a damning indictment of what is wrong in Britain and goes to the core of our political turmoil.

The UK is not alone in facing these challenges. Throughout Europe and the US, profound social, economic, demographic and technological changes are taking place, holding out the prospect of epic consequences for our politics, constitutional structures, democracies and governance. For some, this offers an overdue shake-up of traditional political and establishment elites and the chance to talk about making everything 'great' again, taking our country back and making 'immigration' the real concern. For others, however, there are concerns about a retreat into a darker place where respect for tolerance, difference, inclusion, internationalism and multiculturalism is replaced by authoritarianism, populism, isolationism and a trickle-down form of racism and nationalism. A new battle of ideas is certainly under way but with little consensus as to where we might end up. To paraphrase Shakespeare's *Hamlet*, something is rotten in the state of Britain.

This book attempts to find out what is going on and to work out why our governance, democracy and politics are at risk. Its title is based on Political Action Committee (PAC), a lobbying and major funding group in the US, founded in 1988 to promote corporate interests, socially conservative causes and candidates who support 'limited government, freedom of enterprise, strong families and national sovereignty and security'. These super PACs act as shadow political parties, accept unlimited donations from billionaire corporations and use the money to buy advertising, most of it negative and of the extreme right. This PAC, called Citizens United, also won a now infamous victory in the US Supreme Court where they argued a case on the legal concept of 'corporate personhood', so that corporations could receive the same protections as individuals. This opened the floodgates to corporations building power over the political process, massively corrupting the already fragile democracy in the US and intensifying the marketisation of politics by spending obscene levels of finance.

This power came at the expense of people and is a symptom of the longstanding threat posed to US democracy by the rich and powerful on the right of US politics. The US Supreme Court, the most political court in any western democracy, changed how money could be spent in elections in what is widely regarded as the most regressive piece of legislation in post-war America and a major assault on the rights of the people that confirms the triumph of the market over democracy. This book is intended as a reminder of the power of money and the market in our democracies. It expresses the alternative view that citizens, not corporations or companies, should decide who governs. It makes a plea for the reinvention of our politics, the strengthening of our democracy through effective and responsive governance based on an enhanced and respected role for the citizen. The election of Donald Trump and the arrival of Brexit have added urgency to this idea. Our politics, democracy and governance are holding Britain back.

Setting the Scene Amidst Turbulent Politics

THE WINDS OF political change are blowing through western democracies. The infamous spirit of recent political times is a reminder of the darker political days we thought had gone forever. It is a wake-up call to progressives who believe that humans are capable of achieving much higher levels of social, economic, political and cultural wellbeing. As Naomi Klein says in her new book, *No is Not Enough: Defeating the New Shock Politics*, 'Trump, as extreme as he is, is less an aberration than a logical conclusion – a pastiche of pretty much all the worst and most dangerous trends of the past half century'.

The early years of the 21st century have erupted into a spectacular period of seismic political unrest which challenges our sense of purpose, shreds our certainties, and questions our path to progress in the post-war era. Volatile and angry electors are contesting social democracy and progressive politics. Populism, the rise of the right and the angry backlash of 'left behinds' are dominating politics at a time of unprecedented and accelerating change in every dimension of society.

My argument is that there is something profoundly wrong with our politics, democracy and governance that is impacting on the way we live and how we organise our society. This period of political turmoil demands a positive and progressive response and requires us to dig deeper to find out what populism means and how this is changing our politics.

I believe that the decision to leave the EU was a mistake, and we must examine why this happened and what the catastrophic consequences are likely to be. There is a need to contest, derail and ultimately defeat this act of collective self-harm, which has no benefits for Britain and is tearing the country, government and politics apart. As this nightmare engulfs us, countless important political issues are being cast aside – climate change, inequality, education, older people, homelessness and housing conditions (especially after the Grenfell tragedy in London), while Westminster gets down to work on seven new Bills, over an extended two-year period, to pave the way for Britain to leave the EU.

This makes no sense. Outside this country, people believe we have taken leave of our senses. Enough is enough. A new campaign is needed to make Britain sane again and win the EU back for Britain.

The future of Scotland is bigger than nationalism, populism or the SNP. I want to see Labour engage, interact with a wider audience and argue for federalism, acknowledging that the constitutional question will not go away and accepting the simple truth that if the SNP didn't exist, we would still need a radical shake-up of the structure of the UK and a reassessment of Scotland's role in it.

Over the last decade, Scotland has lacked choice because of the dominance of the SNP, the refusal of Labour to offer a viable and sustainable alternative and the intense disinterest of Westminster, which may ultimately determine the destiny of Scotland. Whether Scotland becomes independent is still a very live question. Despite the SNP's momentum slowing, the stacking up of problems for the Scottish Government and party discipline being so rigid are preventing any debates on issues and new ideas. There now exists a set of factors which could change the dynamic of when a second independence referendum might take place and present Scots with a different choice. Brexit, which has overwhelmed and distracted everyone, has the potential to be a total game changer. With none of the other parties offering a convincing constitutional alternative, the actual reality of leaving the EU – and the devastating impact on Scotland if that happens – will change the parameters of the economic case for independence.

The behaviour of the present Tory government might be enough to reignite the Scotland question. There is no settled will of the Scottish people and the clear question thrown up by the Brexit fiasco is, what would constitute one? The lessons of the EU referendum should be ringing in our ears. Delivering the destiny of a nation is no easy task. There must be a much wider debate which transcends the tribal politics that characterise Scotland today. Old unionism does not begin to rise to the challenges of an aspirational Scotland or the circumstances of a bitterly divided and declining Union. So, the battle will be between a federal structure or independence. Independence is up and running. Federalism is barely at the starting gate. This is the challenge for Labour. Within the context of Westminster's proven inability to reform itself over centuries, can federalism move from being a theoretical but inspirational option, to a runner as a constitutional future for Scotland? The odds on this happening are long, but the fact that so many Scots remain unconvinced by independence, after a decade of SNP dominance, suggests there is a future for a new idea.

'What's the matter with the UK?' is a valid question that needs answering as its post-war decline continues, bitter divisions are reinforced and a dangerous, delusional and sentimental embrace of the past threatens its stability, undermining any sense of solidarity and putting at risk the existence of the Union in its present form.

The divisive, dysfunctional two-party politics of the US requires urgent treatment as the marketisation of US politics expands. Trump has only made matters worse. The Pledge of Allegiance is likely to see 'one nation under God' replaced with 'one nation under the market' and the Gettysburg address adapted to read 'for, by and of the lobbyists'.

The lack of a written constitution for the UK empowers Westminster at the expense of the people, starves the nations of the UK any real power, encourages political tribalism, perpetuates the myth of absolute sovereignty, weakens and devalues our democracy and undermines effective governance.

The future of our politics and democracy require us to do more than defeat Trump and Brexit, confront right wing populism and rebuild a progressive centre-left agenda. We need to address fundamental questions of how money and market involvement are damaging and distorting our democracy. We need to achieve a healthy fit between market capitalism and democracy and work towards re-establishing the idea of the common good.

We need, above all else, to create a new vision of the 'citizen', where consumers and consumerism give way to citizens and citizenship, and where the qualities of the new citizen give rise to a more active and mature democracy, a deeper form of politics and eventually more representative and collaborative governance. Living by the mantras that 'greed is good' and 'financial wealth is worth' results in people serving money instead of the opposite, and this distracts us from more important issues.

Early Politics and Enduring Values:
Pits, Pulpit, Pitches and Politics

The early years, it was so easy then. The building blocks of a progressive narrative were just part of life and living. The turbulent and troubled politics of the early 21st century are in sharp contrast to my early experiences in the mining community of Methil, Fife in the 1950s and '60s. Pits, Pitches, Pulpit, and Politics influenced and helped shape my life. Mining communities were tough but honest places, immersed in the values of solidarity, social justice, the common good, fairness and a broader humanity: the values that some people would wish us to give up on. This is not just a walk down memory lane, indulging in the sentiment or nostalgia of a bygone era where, viewed through the prism of the unprecedented political upheavals of today, life seemed to be kinder, more thoughtful, and compassionate.

These insights, into the social, political, and economic conditions of a Fife mining community have so much to teach us about fairness, respect for others and the ideas of community and social coherence. Football, politics, mining and the voice of the church were very much part of the community, strengthening the social fabric, reinforcing enduring civic values and constantly asserting the dignity of people. In a world of bewildering political change, it is worth remembering that there are values, ethics and principles that have no need to change. In one way or another, this was the Labour party at work. Labour and the community were inextricably linked with mutual respect, only the Communist party providing political opposition. The public was intimately involved in politics. Labour politics with its 'socialist Sunday schools' was identified with the church. Evangelical Christians, the Trades Unions, the Co-operative Movement and a multitude of other organisations, including football clubs, contributed to a sense of community, class consciousness and the idea of the common good. There is much to learn from the politics of the past as we seek new ways today of building better futures.

My family were deeply involved in the Labour party and the various organisations that dominated daily life.

The Glenrothes seat, as it is now named – my old parliamentary constituency – was a red stronghold for 80 years, including a Communist MP, Willie Gallagher, from 1935 to 1951. The year of the 100th anniversary of the death of Keir Hardie would have been a good year to carry on this tradition, but like every other Labour seat in Scotland, bar one, it fell to the SNP on 7 May 2015.

Born and brought up in the Methil area, knocking doors in election campaigns was for me like a walk down memory lane. My 30 years in elected politics, including my 14 years at Westminster, are all linked to this parliamentary seat. My father and grandfather were miners at the nearby Wellesley Colliery. My mother worked at the Co-op store in an area where the 'divi' (the Co-op dividend) was the real currency. She later became Labour party branch secretary in nearby Kennoway. My grandparents lived near Keir Hardie Street in Methil. My grandmother was a member of the Labour party and the Co-op party for over 60 years and worked alongside my grandfather in the soup kitchens in the 1926 miner's strike. Like myself, my grandfather played for the local football team, East Fife, whose old stadium was literally along the street. After returning from the First World War, shocked and traumatised by his experiences, he became an evangelical Christian. He talked a lot about the common good; the fact that after 1900 working people were represented in Parliament; and that the private mines in which he worked were taken into public ownership and safety regulations were introduced. The trauma of the First World War and the story of trenches full of dead bodies made the idea of a decent life for everyone so important. His Christian faith was always founded on the poor, the vulnerable and the ideas of compassion and solidarity. Are these values any less relevant today? Why have they lost their significance in modern times?

Born a few hundred yards from Keir Hardie Street, it was difficult not to inherit a sense of real belonging and become absorbed by political history and family ties. We live in different times but there is still a powerful and enduring set of values, principles and ethics that can be harnessed to improve the lives of people, provide the soul of a new progressive politics and create a mood for radical change.

The powerful community forces at work in Methil were the same forces which created Labour party in 1900: trades unionism, evangelical Christianity, the Independent Labour party and the Co-op movement. It espoused the cause of working people – the common good, tackling inequality, creating a fair and just society and defending people in the workplace.

Labour was built on a broad coalition of interests. The world has changed, and 102 years after Keir Hardie's death, there is much for us to reflect upon. The Labour party had won the respect and confidence of people and were credible and relevant to what was going on. Labour was of the people and the community – 'of them, by them and for them'. Being Labour was as easy as breathing.

Being optimistic about the complex issues of today is a tough ask. Change isn't easy. But in a period of profound disquiet about our politics and the seismic upheavals in our democracy and governance, we need to make sense of what is happening, explore new and better ways of engaging with each other and find new ideas for tackling the myriad of problems and opportunities in this world of unrelenting and unprecedented upheaval. The past has a great deal to teach us. A society with soul and substance will allow people to feel they have control of their lives and influence over what is happening around them. This loss of control and the feeling of exclusion are undermining personal confidence and paving the way for assaults such as Trump and Brexit to win success.

Social Democracy in Crisis:
The Rise of Populism and the Political Right

In western democracies, the pillars of post-war politics – security, stability, solidarity, social cohesion and social mobility – are under threat. The wind of change is getting stronger. The questioning and contesting of the traditional is intensifying. A new consciousness is stirring and complaining. The post-war political settlement is in danger of being torn up. A new era has emerged where anger, angst, uncertainty, insecurity, fear, grievance and resentment are changing the opinions of millions of people. The agony and humiliation of feeling you are losing out or falling behind are increasingly shaping the face of our politics, which in turn is weakening democracies and delivering ineffective governance. The heretical is becoming the commonplace. Many are looking for a new future that offers hope and populism is capturing the minds of those who feel politically excluded. Populists and the right have corralled and exploited much of this revolt. Progressives see this as a step back into a darker past and as a direct threat to social democracy, socialism and liberal democracy. They see freedoms and progressive policies under attack in a populist backlash that reminds them of the uglier parts of history and the myriad evils which accompany authoritarianism, intolerance, economic nationalism and right wing extremism. In the sweep of modern political history, is this transitory or transformational? A tipping point or a blip? Background noise or clear signals of a new normal being formed?

The context. The forces shaking and transforming the old political order are globalisation, automation, technology, the digital revolution, the Facebook era, the marketisation of society, the economy and politics, austerity (the ongoing effect of the financial crisis of 2008), the atomisation of society and the rise of individualism. Deepening inequality and the decline of social democracy and progressiveness are scarring our societies and crowding out hope for the future. Populism offers the past in a new garb.

The events. Brexit 2016, the Scottish referendum 2014, the US presidential election and the migrant crisis in the EU. Trump 2016, Macron/Le Pen 2017, Wilders 2017 and the 2015 and 2017 UK general elections and the 2017 constitutional referendum in Turkey.

The causes. People falling behind, being excluded, feeling that no one is listening; the breakdown of traditional loyalties and allegiances; the entitlements of elites; and mainstream parties taking people for granted; erosion of respect resulting in a backlash from the 'just about managing'.

The emotions. Especially in England, a sense of frustration, anxiety, loss of control and influence, nostalgia, longing for past conditions (real or imaginary) the lure and the loss of greatness, a sense of not belonging in a changing nation, fewer landmarks directions and signposts, fear of the unknown, heightened social anxieties, real material deprivation for many (both in or out of work). One grievance runs into another, anger and grudge become more combustible and people are receptive to emergent 'heroes' who appear empathetic, offering hope and a direction in which to channel grievances and blame as an outlet for their anger. Trump and Brexit exhibit all of these. The idea of the 'political fan' is emerging where 'we will support you evermore' becomes a powerful mantra from the tribal world of football.

The reactions. Anger towards establishment elites and experts with hostility to traditional parties in some quarters, identity and nationality politics shaping the debate and the scapegoating and 'outing' of people, difference becoming a focus for anger. Groups of people or someone or something blamed for our national decline.

The conclusions or outcomes. A new extremism – of the left, but mainly of the right. Profound dissatisfaction with the way people feel they are being treated. A fragile and uncertain politics, the emergence of intolerance and a new era of 'isms' threatening the political space and undermining what was a fragile consensus. Fake news, fraud news, alternative facts, the post-truth debate and the lying press (all of which have overtones of the conditions under pre-war nationalist regimes in Europe), are in danger of destroying the basis of rational and constructive debate. This is politics without a trusted base of facts and evidence, where consensus crumbles and each political base develops its own parallel universe.

The exploiters. The constellation of populists, the right, the treacherous, the cheap patriots who say they love their country (but do everything to damage it), the ideologues, all the 'isms' and racism. The media (especially the right-leaning press) engaging millions of people by ostensibly offering to reflect their emotions, patriotism and love of country, but in reality encouraging them to vote against their own economic interests, abusing truth on an industrial scale and promoting right wing fanaticism as common sense and in the best interests of the country. The press has moved from giving commentary to becoming key players in the unfolding of any political drama.

The enemy within. The mindset of the right in the Conservative party, delusional extremists and fanatical ideologues in Government and Cabinet. (We need to smell the coffee and accept there is a political enemy within – in some cases encouraged by right wing tabloids, often shunned as inappropriate by broadcasters, ignored and nurtured in equal measures by the Tory leadership, seldom on the radar screen of the public and often obscured by Oxbridge accents, elite backgrounds and plausible and intelligent narratives. We hear about the hard left but never the hard right!)

The consequences. A Union and politics in decline, bitter social and economic issues, the cumulative effect of post-war decline being a disunited kingdom with no sense of national purpose – 'four nations' a lie, but not recognised.

The depth of this social fracture was captured by Benjamin Disraeli – Conservative prime minister and novelist – in *Sybil: Or the Two Nations*. Referring specifically to the divide between the rich and the poor in 19th century Britain, he wrote:

Two nations; between whom there is no intercourse and no sympathy; who are ignorant of each other's habits, thoughts and feelings, as if they were dwellers in different zones, or inhabitants of different planets; who are formed by a different breeding, are fed by different food and are ordered by different manners, and are not governed by the same laws.

Money, ideology and the highly destructive advance of the market into the social and public realms are dividing today's Britain. Politics is no longer out in the open. A market economy is fast becoming a market society where no alternative narrative of public philosophy exists.

Our Democracy is Weak and Ineffective

For the majority of people, voting is their only link with the complex structure of democracy, politics and governance that helps shape our society and makes sense of the tough process of arriving at collective decisions out of a bewildering array of multiple and competing interests, opinions, ideas and lifestyles.

The Greek words 'demos' (people) and 'kratos' (power), combine in the word democracy to become symbolic of an inspiring and powerful but remarkably difficult idea to deliver. It was Abraham Lincoln in his Gettysburg address who said, 'government of the people, by the people, for the people, shall not perish from this earth'.

How do these lofty ideals reflect what is happening at Westminster, post election? How can a Conservative party with 29 per cent of the eligible votes cast on 8 June 2017 form a Government? Why do 60 per cent of those who did vote, but voted for other parties, end up having little influence on how Britain is run in the next five years? Can it be right that the Democratic Unionist Party (DUP) with only 279,000 votes and 10 seats, be influential in shaping the future of Britain's future?

More to the point, we are seeing Government of the party, by the party, for the party, where narrow partisan party politics eclipse any notion of the national interest, further diminish the credibility of our democracy, allowing an 'elected dictatorship' to function; 71 per cent of all voters did not support the Conservatives or the DUP. The injustices and inconsistencies of our electoral system run deep.

The struggle for universal suffrage, the right to vote, was a great victory for working people and remains the most important means at their disposal to influence their own lives, the fortunes of their families and indeed the course of history.

Despite the efforts of the Whigs and Tories and the 'nobles, burgesses, and shire commissioners' before them, the struggle for universal voting rights became unstoppable, but was only completely achieved in 1969. For the founding fathers in the US and the privileged classes in Britain, extending the franchise was fraught with fear of the people, rather than power of the people. The idea of 'mobocracy' and the 'behaviour of the masses' was a threat to elites.

In the modern era, the 'first past the post' system for Westminster elections is archaic, politically repressive, unfair and unrepresentative. The lack of a written constitution means that absolute power remains with Westminster, not the people. The younger generation is crying out to be listened to, but Westminster will not extend the franchise or give a voice to 16-year-olds. The ideas of consensus, cooperation, and coalition, unlike Europe, are not part of the Westminster discourse. Proportional representation would help fix our broken politics, strengthen a weak democracy and tackle the remoteness of governance.

Reforming the voting system for Westminster is, however, not on the agenda. The status quo has preserved the dominance of Labour and the Conservatives, reinforced partisanship and, despite the emergence of a multi-party system, made millions of votes worthless in terms of political impact and fairness. This is a rigged system.

Continental Europe is showing the way forward. Post-war forms of proportional voting have overcome much of the tribalism that is still the hallmark of Westminster, and has resulted in a better match between votes cast, political party representation, the composition of government and successful coalitions.

The defeat of the modest 'Alternative Vote' system in a referendum in 2011 is only of significance to the point that this was a sham, a concession to the Lib Dems in the Tory Coalition, with little support from the two major parties. Voting is a powerful and undervalued democratic right in Britain. Often the media, right wing politicians and those obsessed with the 'market' ignore the importance of our democracy, our politics, and our governance. They remain content with first past the post, a system which dominates and distorts the consequences of voting and ensures millions of votes don't matter.

The American author Mark Twain once quipped, 'if voting made any difference, they wouldn't let us do it'. In Britain, millions of people may have taken this to heart. From 1997, 30 to 40 per cent of the electorate haven't bothered to vote in Westminster elections. In 2015, the SNP won 50 per cent of the vote but picked up 95 per cent of the seats in Scotland.

In similar vein, UKIP received nearly 4 million votes and only one MP. This doesn't make any sense. The Tory victory in the 2015 General Election meant they formed the Government with just over a third of the votes cast and only slightly over a quarter of those eligible to vote in the UK. This was repeated in the 2017 General Election. There is now an undeniable case for change: the worth of a vote and the value of voting are at stake.

In today's volatile political climate, the political, social, economic and cultural challenges demand a more inclusive, fairer, representative system of voting. Our politics are crying out for a civilised approach, co-operation, progressive coalitions and consensus. It beggars belief that in 2017 we hold on to the ideas that each manifesto is unique and precious, that each party has a monopoly of wisdom to solve every problem and that supporting or working with another party is a sign of weakness. People don't think like this. This is not the European way. First past the post only reinforces this state of delusion.

But change is difficult. The status quo serves the self-interest of the two big parties. Their case against change is plausible but flawed. Simplicity, speed, MP–voters link, decisive results and strong and stable government, are seen as advantages.

First past the post has substantial weaknesses: MPs and governments elected without majority votes; parties that win large numbers of votes but obtain few seats; and smaller parties under-represented or not represented in the House of Commons. Key institutions of our democracy – parties, parliaments, and elections – do not command enough trust or respect.

Our politics and our electoral system are not coping. Proportional representation voting, votes for 16-year-olds to give them a greater say in the intergenerational debate and transferring power to the people in a written constitution, are long overdue. Voters are serious people. As citizens, not consumers, they recognise the fact that politics, democracy, and governance have profound consequences for their lives. Abandoning first past the post for Westminster elections is the next step in the struggle for voting rights. Let's learn from Europe.

The worth of a vote should never be underestimated or abused.

Citizens and citizenship have become a convenient administrative label. For many people, their experience of democracy and politics is relegated to an outing to the polling station, at least for the 60 to 70 per cent of the public who use their vote in general elections. It is remarkable that our Parliament at Westminster seems unconcerned that 30 to 40 per cent of the population never vote. Maybe people have woken up to the notion that nothing will change.

The struggle for the universal franchise was a tough battle with the Whigs and Tories in Westminster. For many people, voting at the polling station seems more like a validation of the process than a real opportunity to shape the future of the country. Politics has become an end, rather than a means to a much wider set of social and economic objectives.

2

The New Political Landscape

VISITING THE SUPREME Court in Washington, where the body of Justice Antonin Scalia was lying in repose, I was reminded of the significance and importance of this constitutional court to the lives of ordinary US citizens. In sharp contrast, I thought of the so-called 'British constitution', which is in crisis. Of course there is no written constitution. That is why we had a referendum on Britain's membership of the EU. It wasn't so much about the important challenges facing either Britain or the EU but more to do with a civil war within the Conservative party. It was just another example of the near total power now exercised by the House of Commons and, for the next five years, the Conservative party. This may be the logical outcome of our parliamentary democracy, where the winner takes all. But for how much longer can the British people be at the mercy of a ramshackle set of conventions, rules, regulations and laws created over a thousand years ago, masquerading as a constitution and resulting in the poor governance of Britain, the rights, liberties and freedoms of every citizen lacking effective recognition and protection, and the needs of four distinct nations being consistently downplayed and marginalised. Our archaic system is not working. There are few checks or balances in our constitutional framework and the EU referendum debate exposed the key priority of the Government: the safeguarding of the absolute sovereignty of the Conservative party, rather than that of the British people.

This was recently described as an 'omni-competent centralised executive constrained only by periodic popular elections'. This is an increasingly dysfunctional and disrespected political system. There is also a growing and damaging imbalance of power between the institutions of the state itself.

Lord Hailsham described this in 1976 as an 'elective dictatorship'. This is a more accurate description today. Governments are increasingly inclined to introduce fundamental constitutional changes, many of which are effectively irreversible and are unwilling to respect the independent authority of the judiciary, the civil service, local government, parliament itself and the legislatures of the other nations in the UK. Post-devolution, the importance of our four nation politics continues to be undervalued and often marginalised. Our relationship with the EU remains fractious and fragile to the extent that, since our accession to membership in 1975, we have totally failed to factor in the reality that nation state power has been ceded and there is no such thing as the absolute sovereignty of the Westminster Parliament. We are living in a post-sovereign multination and interdependent world. In a very large number of democratic states, a codified written constitution specifies and guarantees the relationships between the various organisations of the state and their respective powers.

Our historic and uncodified constitution has evolved in a haphazard manner, failing to provide respect for different parts of our constitutional framework and at the same time failing to secure any concessions from Westminster about the legitimacy of the new ways of running a modern Britain.

The government at Westminster acted as if it were 1916 not 2016. The referendum had little to do with the real challenges facing Britain and the EU. The true nature of the referendum was illustrated by the leadership antics of the former Mayor of London who saw the whole exercise through the prism of his ambitions, so the future of Britain became less important than the future of Boris: what a fiasco.

The single dictatorship of the Conservative party in the House of Commons is operating without any constitutional safeguards or effective or proper scrutiny. Democracy itself is being undermined as the Government moves to undermine electoral registration, deny votes to 16-year-olds, promote boundary changes for political gain and destroy the rights of trades unionists. These are matters that should require a debate and the consent of a constitutional discussion extending well beyond the narrow and increasingly partisan confines of the House of Commons. This is what happens in other countries, why not in Britain?

A constitution would have set out the parameters of whether or not a referendum should be necessary on issue of public concern. We are fast approaching the point where British people need to be protected from the excesses of Governments between elections. So with no consent other than a mention in a manifesto, a referendum on the EU was pushed through the House of Commons: the public interest played second fiddle to the interest of the party. We seem to be fast becoming political subjects engaged in elections but excluded from ongoing involvement because there is no constitution to reflect the importance of the public will. What ever happened to the Abraham Lincoln idea that the survival of representative democracy requires, 'that government of the people, by the people, for the people, shall not perish'? The Conservatives want subjects and consumers but Britain needs citizens.

The EU referendum is only one illustration of a uniquely British constitutional mess. Our electoral system is at breaking point. Defending the historical privileges of the two main parties at Westminster makes no sense. Examples make the case for reform. UKIP poll 4 million votes and get one MP, the SNP poll 1.4 million votes and get 56 MPs. Labour should lead the campaign for change. The House of Lords is a remarkable relic of past privilege and patronage and to a great extent still is. Its' abolition is long overdue. Four nation politics and devolved government is still viewed by some as a concession to political pressure and not as the basis for a way forward for modern Government and the unity of Britain. A new written constitution would safeguard our membership of the EU by creating a proper constitutional court as in Germany and the US and put the jurisdiction of the European Court of Human Rights and the protections of the European convention beyond the reach of partisan politics.

Britain needs a constitution to save us from the arbitrary decisions of a one party government. The sovereignty of the people does matter.

Towards a New Order:
Building a New Consensus For Progressives

In this political upheaval, many questions remain unanswered. The Scotland Question: a nation in transition but where is it going? Has the SNP bubble burst after dominating Scottish politics for over a decade? Or will Brexit, the Tories and Westminster ensure the volatility of politics in a Scotland now embracing identity, nationality and populism? Is Independence the only alternative to a declining Union or can genuine federalism capture the imagination of Scots as a serious, sustainable, and supportable way forward?

Reinventing the Labour party – unchanging principles in changing times. Can the Corbyn bounce, in particular Labour's manifesto in the 2017 general election, give credibility, relevance and radicalism to the Labour party? A new role for Labour is opening up. The Tories are struggling to adapt to a different kind of politics and presiding over a shambolic and out of touch government. It is worth bearing in mind, however, the remarkable resilience of a Conservative party whose instincts for survival are legend.

To use a Trumpism, can Britain be Great Again or is a declining, divided, and disunited Union, destined to deteriorate further as today's turbulent and troubled politics take their toll and Brexit further diminishes our international role, reputation and influence? A more important question for this book is whether people can be great and be more influential in shaping their own lives and their country.

After celebrating its 60th birthday in 2017, can the EU build on its remarkable achievements of peace, prosperity, and progress, and secure a more successful, and stable future? The EU will always be an antidote to the excesses of nationalism and, in the future, the antithesis of the economic nationalism, isolationism and nativism that the empty rhetoric of, 'taking our country back' seems to stand for. Brexit was a mistake, a massive exercise in national self-harm. Can we create in the country a campaign to remain, which boosts the resolve of the natural majority of MPs at Westminster to stay in the EU and promote the real benefits of winning Europe back for Britain? This is a new battle for Britain to remain in the EU.

Transforming Politics

The power of ideas must drive our politics. Populism brings back the cult of personality which, in the case of the US and Turkish presidents, represents the worst aspects of authoritarianism, intolerance and the sacrificing of mainstream ideas and respect. Our politics have become focused on individual leadership to the exclusion of ideas, policy and philosophy. This allows the media to debate and concentrate on what a party leader does rather than what his or her party is offering. For progressives, removing Theresa May as Conservative party leader is of little significance because the threat to Britain comes from the Conservative party and not from whoever is their leader at any moment in time.

We need to get back to concentrating on what a party stands for and be less involved in the intrigue of leadership contests. Of course, the qualities of a party leader count, especially in this world of 24-hour news cycles and social media, but ideas are more important for Britain and the public. We need to rescue our politics and present a different approach to discussing the issues that really matter and diminish the importance of our obsession with personality to the exclusion of all else.

Democracy at Risk

Democracy is as a system of government with four key elements:

- A political system for choosing and replacing the government through free and fair elections.
- The active participation of the people, as citizens, in politics and civic life.
- Protection of the human rights of all citizens.
- A rule of law in which the laws and procedures apply equally to all citizens.

The reality of these demands may be very different from these laudable intentions, and that is why power of people in the form of the citizen needs to be invented. Citizens need more than votes and more than walk on parts in elections. Voting so often appears to be the validation of a process rather than the reflection of real citizen involvement. There is also a generational divide within society. Are there early signs in Britain of the Tories mimicking the despicable practices of voter suppression which are becoming so prevalent in the southern states of the US under the Republicans? Donald Trump has established a commission in the US to develop the case for more draconian measures to extend the idea of keeping hostile voters away from polling stations. Do we understand the sacrifice and struggle behind the fight for universal suffrage? Are the excesses of the market compatible with democracy?

The Citizen

A political trinity of citizen, political building blocks and foundations, and powerful and enduring ideas could transform the way we approach and conceive what is relevant to the needs and aspirations of people, and the monumentally important issues that are not receiving the attention they deserve. The focus on the citizen is the key to winning back control of a failing democracy and ensuring more effective and responsive governance at every level.

The shock politics and troubled and tumultuous times of the early millennium demand new thinking and innovation. Britain needs to transform politics to improve lives and deal with the profound questions and ideas that underpin the building of a tolerant, inclusive, equal, and just society. At the heart of this must be a new role for citizens in our democracy: this is the opportunity for citizens to reclaim their politics and break the rigged system that does not operate in the interests of millions of people. There are four steps to make Britain's politics better, re-energise progressive parties and put citizens in the forefront of our efforts. This has to be a rebirth of our politics.

First, we need to create a greater synergy and bond between our politics, our democracy and our governance and reassert the importance of people.

Second, using the ambitious headline of *Citizens United* we need to spell out what a different kind of society would be like and identify the building blocks or foundations needed to construct such a new and ambitious project. The ideas and the vision that have shaped our thinking from Athenian Greece to the Gettysburg address to the fall of the Berlin Wall to the creation of the European Union in 1957, and which have sought to define how societies should evolve and shape the quality of life of their citizens, have to be revisited. We need to debate and develop ideas that have existed throughout history but which have been overwhelmed, lost or side-lined in modern times; not because they are unimportant or irrelevant but because of the systematic erosion of the public space and the political, media and economic pressures to elevate a more soulless market philosophy above all other considerations. The transformation of our political and public discourse is long overdue.

Third, we need to establish the framework of building blocks which would form the foundations of this citizen's renaissance and the rebuilding of progressive politics:

- Creating a public philosophy as the basis of a new narrative.
- Establishing the idea of equal worth.
- Confronting the market and its relentless incursion into social and public realms.
- Halting the marketisation of our democracy; money, markets and the lack of morality are deepening inequality and undermining the strength of our democracy.
- Looking beyond individuality.
- Rethinking our notion of the 'Acquisitive Society'.
- Developing a broader humanity.
- Promoting the primacy of the idea of the Common Good.
- Acknowledging that inequality is poisoning the well of society and the need to tackle its highly disruptive and divisive effects on the effective functioning and fairness of modern life.
- Addressing the future of work and its distribution in society and the consequences of Automation, Artificial Intelligence, and Robotics and in particular the relationship between, labour, capital, and employment in the 21st century.

Fourth, building on these foundations, how do we develop the big idea of the citizen being at the heart of this renaissance and what areas of interest do we need to consider for this to happen? This is the agenda for change:

Re-imagining our politics and democracy. For many, our politics seem to be regressing and drifting further away from the idealism and vision of earlier times. Looking towards the future, a more inclusive political debate must re-imagine our politics and democracy for modern times, but it has to be focused on the timeless assertion of fundamental human ideals and needs and the dignity of men and women.

Society and the search for meaning. There are many questions being posed about the meaning of modern life and its lack of a political soul. People are looking for some certainty, direction, and reassurances in what has become a troubling world of crises and frightening changes.

Addressing the market. The market, in all its imperfections and its attempt to encroach further on the public and social realms, is undermining our way of life and questioning how people relate and interact with each other. The atomisation of society, often reinforced by the new electronic age, is intensifying. As consumers in the market place we can validate our role at the heart of capitalism by gaining access to credit scores showing how dependable and worthy we are as consumers; corporations and companies can obtain credit ratings. There is no such quality assurance or assessment of people as citizens in our democracy. Being a citizen is more important than being a consumer, but society does not recognise this.

Philosophy matters. Our political debates are dominated by the narratives of the right and their ability to put forward, in simple and straightforward language, plausible but often deeply flawed ideas of where life and society should be heading. By making philosophy accessible and intelligible we can provide a counter blast to the one-sided debates which are disfiguring our politics and distorting our democracy.

Principles and creed in changing times. Britain's political history has never been over-occupied with the doctrinal approach to politics exhibited by other European countries. Instead, principles and creeds have been more important. Again, the question has to be posed, does the progressive left in Britain have a block of principles and a creed which will help people easily understand what the political offering is?

Ethics. What is the right thing to do? This is a question rarely put in our political discourse in Britain. Parties are so busy wrapped up in their exceptionalism and 'unique' body of thought called a manifesto, which seeks to offer electors the wisdom of all the ages in a single volume. No one thinks or acts like a party manifesto. Instead, there should be a recognition of the truths and wisdom of ideas that embrace common sense and the right solution. In the context of majorities and minorities there are complex moral and practical arguments to be settled. Referendums, for example, have become the weapon of political choice. The EU referendum illustrated the dangers of a binary approach to such a huge and emotional issue, which raises the question of when is a majority a real and significant verdict, or is one vote always enough and who decides? Binary mindsets devalue our democracy. If Parliament is sovereign, how can it be bypassed by a referendum? If referendums are consultative, why did Parliament not recognise this? Was Parliament, in terms of the EU referendum, merely dumping on the British people a question too difficult for the Conservative party and Westminster to handle? Perhaps this constitutional farce and catastrophic outcome could have been avoided, had we a written constitution outlining the conditions in which a referendum should be held and how it should be dealt with. Greater civic literacy and more political knowledge would serve to create an informed citizenry and boost a transforming democracy.

Moods and Movements. President Macron was elected in France with a mood and a movement, and no party. People have moods and are now capable of creating movements of the mind as well as mass movements of a practical kind. The era of social media such as Facebook has boosted the idea of political movements, with its ability to create instant issues and points of contact. This raises all sorts of questions for society and its politics. One thing is certain: a movement should never become a 'mob', on the internet or in reality, and a majority should never disrespect or ignore the minority.

Identity. The search for belonging and meaning are recurring themes in a world of change. Multiple identities, at a moment in time, will throw up a dominant identity which could shape our history – Brexit is an example of the power of identity. The Scottish Independence referendum drove millions of Scots to the polls, in the biggest voter turn-out in British electoral history. People, asserting who they are, who they were or who they would like to be, are creating massive moods and swings in what is now a fragile and volatile electorate. Are we still seeking security, stability, solidarity and social coherence in our lives or is a more adventurous future in the making? What did Brexit represent?

Governance of the people, for the people, by the people? What does sovereignty of Westminster mean, if anything, in a world of interconnectedness, interdependency and internationalism? People are anxious about the over-promising of governments and their under-delivery. In Britain, are we heading towards an economic nationalism, European exclusion and further isolationism? Are people or parliaments sovereign? Does Scotland have any real power, or is devolved power limited and controlled by Westminster? Without a written constitution, do people have any real power in Britain?

Constitutionalism: more 21st century, less Magna Carta. Britain's constitution is a disaster. It is not codified, written, accessible or belonging to the people, and thus our unwritten constitution is not fit for 21st century purposes. It is more a statement of the past than a commitment to the future. The elective dictatorship of Westminster carries all before it and, with no power in the land exercising any real or effective controls over what it does, the result is a make it up as you go constitution. Elites argue that there is no need for a written constitution and justify this by claiming the people are not interested in having one. This has never been tested, but it is logical to assume that when the public are totally excluded from a key part of their democracy, they are unlikely to be critical. It remains one of the reasons why Britain is being held back. People are too easily dismissed. Once seen as subjects of the Monarchy, legal entities for everyday life, and consumers in the market-place, the importance of people as citizens, especially in politics and the public realm, has for far too long been ignored. This must change.

What's the point of politics? Our political process, politicians and political parties have achieved a great deal and served Britain well in the post-war era. The politics of the 21st century tell a different story and questions are being asked. Are they fit for purpose? Do they have the ability to deliver? Are political parties too tribal and partisan to deal with modern challenges? Is the political process looking more important than political outcomes? And as progressives, we seem to be incapable or unwilling to co-operate and coalesce around obvious areas of agreement where the common good is staring them in the face. Do Westminster and Washington not confirm how dysfunctional politics has become? They are stages on which party political battles are fought to the death and outcomes arrived at which are likely to be overturned next time round. There is no disputing the fact that politics is complex and that distilling the hopes and aspirations of millions of people into manageable chunks of legislation and executive action is not easy. But, acknowledging the fact that this is now 2017 and not 1917, shouldn't there be a more radical assessment of where we are heading and a reinvention of politics to cope with today and a different future for tomorrow? The question seems appropriate in many ways, but there is the compelling thought that we are simply not able to influence or control social, economic or technological change in the public interest. These forces and changes are outstripping our ability to cope and the speed of change is simply overwhelming us. As a result, we are at the mercy of the consumer market forces with all the consequences that may hold for society and our way of life. Politics may have to leap into another time dimension, so that we can reinvent it, update our thinking and reconfigure what a civilised and compassionate society could look like. Fundamentalism and intolerance in politics, as in religion, will have consequences. Politics, in the eyes of some, should be reduced to a thin veneer dealing with the excesses of the market, while giving the appearance of a civilised and caring society. The more radical ideas should not obscure the need for immediate and practical reforms such as, introducing votes for 16-year-olds, scrapping first past the post elections, willing to accept coalitions, introducing a written constitution and creating a federal structure for the UK.

The citizen is the basic building block of a new way of doing politics in the 21st century. The Athenians believed in them, why shouldn't we? But, as a clash between democracy and the market becomes inevitable, this approach will be difficult. Those with a hankering for past certainties, including right leaning newspapers, will attempt to frustrate progress. Britain has never been a radical country, but the future may be very different from the present. We need a new political renaissance or enlightenment. There are, however, other factors and forces at work who are willing prisoners of the past – Brexit is a powerful illustration of a country taking a huge step backwards, thinking it was progress –

and who would not welcome the idea of citizens united.

In this new millennium, public opinion in the democracies of North America and Western Europe is turning against traditional politics and politicians. While Trump and Brexit may be short-lived nightmares, the millions of people who voted for them are real and need to be respected. The public have never been more mistrustful, disconnected and disillusioned with democracy and governance. Trust between people and politicians has broken down. A quiet revolution simmers. Outcomes are unclear and uncertain. A great deal of bewilderment, fragility and anger has settled on our politics, democracy and governance. The word 'citizen' has lost any significance or symbolism as market capitalism further encroaches on areas of public and social interest far removed from harsh economic climates. In the absence of a progressive narrative or a philosophy to halt the march of these destructive forces in society, this rapidly changing world is likely to slide further into a chaotic free for all. The certainties we have taken for granted are being shredded.

To some, this recalibration was long overdue. For others, there are now stark and unsettling choices to be made about how we want to live in the 21st century. Acknowledging and prioritising the importance of people is the key to a constructive and more fulfilling politics. Amidst the bewildering political changes taking place, we need to reinvent our politics, constitution, democracy and governance to better reflect and more adequately represent the wishes, worth and aspirations of people as citizens. 'Government of the people, by the people, for the people shall not perish from the earth', still remains a powerful idea for citizens and should be our driving force, behind the goals of creating more fulfilling lives for people, building better societies and tackling a growing agenda of global and local problems, issues and opportunities. The use and significance of the word citizen have largely been lost. Its meaning has been buried under an avalanche of labels – consumers, customers, sellers, buyers and investors to describe people in their various roles in society now dominated by market considerations. It is worth reminding ourselves of the more noble nature of what citizenship means: it is the state of being vested with the rights, privileges and duties of a citizen – the character of an individual viewed as a member of society – behaviour defined in terms of duties, obligations and functions of a citizen – the qualities that a person is expected to have as a responsible member of a community.

Citizenship comes from the Latin word for city. Having rights and responsibilities is the key. It is important for the reinvention of politics that we re-establish citizenship above the more market-driven descriptions that are now given to people. It is about people as human beings. Monarchy required people as subjects, markets want consumers, but democracy demands citizens:

People as citizens not just voters who can genuinely, continuously, and consistently influence the political process.

People as citizens not just consumers who can help resist through democratic means the advances of the market into areas of public life where it has no moral right to be, and through collective pressure and power better 'tame' or manage capitalism.

People as active civic partners and citizens not just passive recipients of public or government services, whose lives, aspirations and futures matter and deserve to be listened to.

People as thinking, questioning, concerned, intelligent and inquiring citizens, not just the recipients of election leaflets and often misleading, partisan and low level press coverage designed to satisfy the requirements of outdated campaign methods and vested interests, instead of raising political literacy and civic awareness. Brexit was the ultimate example of lies, half-truths and astonishing distortions.

People as citizens whose equal worth, in the eyes of others and their own sense of self-worth have to be nurtured and respected, to overcome the divisive labelling and social categorisation that currently scars communities.

People as citizens of Scotland and Britain who embrace a broader humanity, a deep sense of global citizenship, Europeanism and international patriotism, in sharp contrast to the narrowing of horizons, narrow nationalisms, isolationism and dislike of difference.

People as citizens who are blind to skin colour, ethnicity, race or religion and who seek common purpose, common fellowship and common ground to build solidarity and a shared sense of social purpose.

People as citizens feeling included, helping shape new political cultures, new creeds and a new politics, adding enormously to the richness of life.

People as citizens, feeling confident in themselves and a sense of belonging to their communities and in their countries.

People as informed citizens can help to reinvigorate our politics, build a more representative democracy and stronger governance. People should have a higher regard as themselves as citizens, seizing the fact that they matter and that the ballot box is the most powerful way of improving their country as well as their own lives. The is the challenge of modern politics.

These sentiments, are captured by Harvard Philosophy professor, Michael Sandel. In his Reith Lecture 2009, 'A New Citizenship', Sandel talks about, 'A New Politics of the Common Good' and argues that we needed to reframe the terms of political debate in two ways. First, a debate about the moral limits of the market, and second, a more robust political discourse which engages more directly with the idea of a 'public philosophy'. These are important arguments, particularly when bearing in mind the emptiness of much of the political debate in Britain today. This would be the starting point for a new politics of the common good. Sandel develops how these themes are connected. He argues that for three decades, the governing philosophy of the US and Britain was defined by the faith that markets are the primary instrument for achieving the public good. In the light of the financial crisis of 2007/8 this faith, he argues, should be contested. The era of market triumphalism has ended, but we have yet to find our way to a new governing philosophy. He recognises this is a challenge, identifying as 'one obstacle to a new public philosophy' as

a persisting assumption from the age of market faith... the idea that the primary purpose of government is to correct what economists call market failure. It's the idea that government should try to replicate the outcomes that competitive markets would produce...

As a governing philosophy, however, the task of correcting market failures is too humble and too narrow. Democratic governance is radically devalued if reduced to the role of handmaiden to the market economy.

Observing that 'the attempt to empty politics of moral controversy may seem to be a way of respecting our differences, but it is actually corrosive of democratic life', Sandel says that 'times have changed. All of which suggests that the time may be right for a new kind of politics – a politics of the common good'.

Politics according to Sandel's vision would look very different from market driven politics, for a politics of the common good invites us to think of ourselves less as consumers, and more as citizens. This is the key to unlocking a different way of making politics matter. Sandel argues that political leaders should bear this in mind when making the case for change. The mutual responsibilities of citizenship are important. 'This is a moral and spiritual project, not only an economic one.' He continues:

In the context of the common good an issue that doesn't get much attention in our politics is inequality. Inequalities of income and wealth are now at levels not seen since the 1930s.

Politicians find it difficult to talk about inequality. We tend to talk about inequality as if the problem were how to redistribute access to private consumption. But the real problem with inequality lies in the damage it does to the civic project, to the common good.

Too big a gap between the rich and poor undermines the solidarity that inclusive society needs. The hollowing out of the public realm makes it difficult to cultivate the sense of community that democratic citizenship requires.

Sandel's ground-breaking lectures propose a greater role for moral argument in public life, and for the need to keep markets in their place. This politics of moral and civic renewal is the key to building decent societies in Scotland, Britain, Europe and the US.

There is an urgent need for us to start this renewal.

The EU Referendum Campaign

The EU referendum campaign is a sad but spectacular reminder of the fragile, volatile and uncertain nature of our democracy and our politics. The shallowness of our democracy has been laid bare. Within a few days, the same was being said about our governance and our constitution. This campaign was a damning indictment of what is wrong in Britain and goes to the core of what this book is about. We need a debate about politics. The EU referendum was not about the EU but was a verdict on a declining, uncertain, and deeply divided Britain, not content with being a team player in Europe but instead winding back to indulge in the past. Brexit was about the state of the UK; nothing more, nothing less.

There are profound and unsettling questions being posed by our decision to leave the EU after 43 years of membership. Many of these questions relate to the decision itself, which will have catastrophic consequences for the UK. Over the next decade, this unique exercise in self-harm will consume valuable energy, time, resources and skills at the expense of addressing real problems; global terrorism threats, tackling inequality and injustice, transforming our health and education services, solving the constitutional problems in the UK and avoiding the exit of Scotland and Northern Ireland from the Union, climate change and the saving of our social and public realms from the onward march of unfettered market capitalism will take a back seat. The EU campaign has blown apart any notion that the UK is a mature, stable, and serious democracy. The most important decision in our post-war history was made in conditions of political uncertainty and chaos, where a party engulfed in an internal civil war and threatened by another party, UKIP, decided to gamble the future of Britain. By enlisting the help of the British people in a completely unnecessary referendum, and then as the 'Brit hits the Fan' a whole government walks away from its responsibilities and embarks on a leadership campaign. Finally, after denials to the contrary, Prime Minister Theresa May decides for narrow partisan reasons to have another general election. Her reasons for calling another election were to smash the Labour party (which spectacularly backfires) and to strengthen her negotiating hand in the Brexit negotiations (which again looks like a massive defeat for her).

Tory Obsession

The Tories have been obsessed with the EU for over a generation. Tory Prime Ministers Major, Cameron and soon Theresa May will have been sacrificed by the actions of the obsessional, fanatical and delusional behaviour of the hard right within the Conservative party. Having failed to kill off the treacherous behaviour of their cheap patriots, the Tories have dragged the British people into their European mess and Brexit is the result. Britain is heading for a catastrophe. Emboldened by Brexit, nearly a third of Tory MPs and substantial sections of Theresa May's Government and Cabinet have a more ambitious agenda in store for Britain. The EU was only a start, but still a significant step towards a market-driven, low taxation, low spend, low welfare, offshore bargain basement vision for Britain. After dumping Europe, Britain seeks to embrace the US in a new Anglosphere. Being the 51st state of the Union might not be too wide of the mark.

The EU campaign and its outcome are reminders of the risks facing our politics and our democracy. This illustrates the potential for negligent or intentional harm inflicted by poor governance, broken politics, treacherous behaviour from cheap patriots and a lack of constitutional safeguards.

Not for democracy or national pride, or Britain's role in the world or for economic progress, did David Cameron launch his reckless EU referendum campaign. His initial strategy was aimed at silencing the ultra-EU extremists and to undermine UKIP. Since UKIP's mission has been accomplished they have faded from the political scene, and now Farage, a fan of showbiz politics, is busy with fake news broadcaster, Fox News, in the US, and has been filmed visiting Trump Tower in Manhattan. A self-proclaimed man of the people, in a gold plated lift. The extremists within the Conservative party now pose the real and present threat to the future of Britain.

Linda Colley, writing in *The Guardian,* addressed the plight of Britain when she said:

> The vote confirmed something else: a sense of bereftness that is disproportionately (though not uniquely) felt in England. Lots of people in that country seem to have opted for Brexit out of a near mystical sense that it would somehow give them their country back. This did not simply stem from worries over immigration.

How do we protect our politics and the public from such cynical abuse of the referendum, in itself a crude, dangerous and potentially divisive weapon of political destruction? Maybe the public have to be protected from their politicians; a written constitution would help!

The Brexit vote only exposed weaknesses in the UK that have been longstanding and which, if left unattended, will continue to diminish the standing of Britain in the world.

Will Brexit be a wake-up call for Britain to address the deep seated and long running issues which run like fault lines through our social and economic landscape and created tremors that have now resulted in a political earthquake. Major crises have often resulted in acts of constitutional and political reinvention. Is there any prospect of this happening in Britain?

This raises concerns about a second referendum in Scotland, or indeed the UK, after the outcome of the negotiations are known. The EU referendum has proven to be a decisive statement about the inability of Britain to settle a question without recriminations and divisions, settling an issue for the long term. For Scotland, will a narrow vote either way allow the nation to move on or merely create the conditions for a 'neverendum'? Of wider significance for politics is the fact that binary questions create binary mindsets. Our weak and shallow politics requires a mature democracy where civic awareness, political literacy, and ideas of the common good are deeply embedded. The EU was a special and successful friend that we never got to know!

Although the EU is highly successful and internationally respected, it is not a perfect institution and remains a work in progress. This was never a campaign about the EU but instead was the playing out of a narrative of a UK in long term decline. A referendum, often sold as the best expression of the will of the people, is better described as a dangerous instrument acting as a lightning rod for grudges and grievances, fears and anxieties. In this case, it was an opportunity for politicians to lie, distort and deceive on an industrial scale and, in doing so, exploit an electorate that had been starved of EU facts and information for over 40 years. It was also where political knowledge, issue awareness, civic literacy and balanced press coverage remained at very low levels of development: this is a wake-up call for a more informed democracy and an engaged electorate that sees people as citizens, not consumers, and sees politics as a vital public need, not a market transaction. Reason and emotion, head and heart, fact and opinion, evidence and conjecture, hope and fear, and anger and calm, represent both combustible feelings and objective analysis. Our political campaigns and debates need both. 'Brexit or Leave' showed an aggressive and contemptuous disregard for the truth and ruthlessly exploited all the obvious aspects of a disunited kingdom.

The Broader Perspective

The UK is not alone in facing these challenges. Throughout Europe and the US, profound social, economic, demographic and technological changes are taking place, holding out the prospect of epic consequences for their politics, constitutional structures, democracies and governance. There are concerns about a retreat into a darker place where respect for tolerance, difference, inclusion, internationalism and multiculturalism, is replaced by authoritarianism, isolationism and a trickle-down form of racism and nationalism. A new battle of ideas is certainly underway but with little consensus as to where this might end up. Regardless of the consequences and outcomes, which will vary by country and continent, the role of people as 'citizens' will have to become a vital part of political renewal.

The Politics of Anger

When we look across the current political landscape, it presents a complex, confused and dispiriting picture. There are the consequences of what could have been a possible Scottish exit from Britain (Scexit) 2014 and the reality of Brexit 2016 for Britain and Scotland; the new era after the 2008 global crash; globalisation and neoliberal austerity. The politics of anger, the decline of leadership and a divided Britain; the rise of populism, nationalism and nativism; disillusion with the politics and parties and the disintegration of traditional loyalties and allegiances. This is a 'them and us' kingdom where sharp differences of race, ethnicity, religion and geography are undermining national cohesion, stability and solidarity.

People, in a deeper, spiritual and more philosophical sense, are searching for more meaning in their lives, increasingly dominated by materialism, money and the excesses of the market. The distribution of wealth, income and opportunity are creating disquieting levels of inequality and injustice. National identity and xenophobia (especially in England) are replacing social class and economic solidarity as the drivers of political change and instability. Computers, technology and social media are redefining our ideas of community and relationships, and revolutionising protest, social action and political organisation in ways barely imagined just a few years ago.

These are voices for progress but also for intolerance. Amid the potential for an electronic mob rule against vulnerable minorities, there is a growing sense of apprehension, anger and pessimism and diminishing expectations and aspirations among young people. In large swathes of the old industrial parts of Britain, people feel marginalised and excluded from any notion of a better tomorrow. Increasingly disillusioned by the old politics, they see their traditional ways of living, earning and existing threatened. There is anger and alienation resulting from austerity and the behaviour of elites in a union divided and in decline. All this, along with the political reawakening of England, is doing a great deal to further unsettle Scots and, in this fragile constitutional stand-off, reinforcing for many people the wisdom of leaving the UK.

These issues are combining to form the most formidable challenge in post-war history. Something appears to have gone seriously wrong at the start of the 21st century. People in western democracies have become disillusioned with traditional politics, disconnected from institutions and despairing of the ability of political parties to tackle their concerns.

In Britain, as in some other countries of Western Europe, the search for self-determination and the growing influence of national identity adds another layer of concern and contention and doubt to an already bewildering array of national challenges and public anxiety. The hesitant arrival of 'four nation' politics in the UK, the decline of Britishness, the stirring of England, the rise of national identity as a salient political influence and the decision to leave the European Union, are destined to shake up the constitutional structure of the UK. We are a country still searching for a role in the world, an old politics not fit for purpose and which has lost the confidence of the people.

Helping To Shape Our Thinking and Ideas

Britain needs to focus on a number of priorities:

- on the importance of politics, in terms of its relevance to the modern age
- on democracy (from the Greeks, power of the people), why it matters and what needs to be done to resist the intrusion of market principles
- on our constitutional set up in the UK where a lack of a written, codified and accessible constitution allows Westminster and politicians to take major decisions based on narrow political considerations rather than in the public
- on governance where outdated practices, archaic procedures and declining public support are the result of institutional failure;
- on what next for the UK after the decision to leave the EU and the prospects of Scotland once again revisiting the idea of leaving the UK (Scexit)
- on what a vision for an independent Scotland could look like
- on federalism as an alternative way forward for Scotland;
- on a reinvented Labour party
- on the growing divergence of Scottish and English politics
- on whether the UK, Westminster and the British Conservatives and Labour parties, could ever deliver an alternative constitutional settlement
- on the possibility that the Brexit may never happen.

Britain, Brexit and Scotland: New Ideas

Scotland, in or out of the UK, and Britain, in or out of the EU, are likely to be of remarkable and unprecedented significance for the country as a whole in the next decade.

What kind of future does the Labour party have in Scotland? Although it reversed its fortunes in the 2017 general election, can the Labour party in Scotland continue to recover, reinvent itself and once again, offer a sustainable, credible, relevant and radical alternative to nationalism and Conservatism to win back Scots to social democracy or democratic socialism? Labour has to engage enthusiastically with the constitutional question – which will not go away. Independence will not be defeated by denying Scots the right to vote on the issue. There must be an acceptance that, if the SNP didn't exist, there would still have to be a radical transformation of how the UK is governed. This is Labour's opportunity. If Scots want to stay in the UK then a federal solution must be debated and emerge as a serious option. What is clear is that more devo unionism is not a credible option. The Tories recent run of form in Scotland may evaporate as the fortunes of Theresa May's government at Westminster decline. This is a time of massive uncertainty as Brexit casts a long shadow and austerity cuts continue to undermine the Scottish economy. A hard Brexit is likely to revive the fortunes of independence as people in Scotland face a real choice of being in Europe or being in the UK. This could have a profound effect on the mood of Scotland.

Can the SNP retain its dominance of Scotland, despite its recent setbacks, loss of momentum and policy difficulties? Never a party of the left, does its signature policy of Independence have the strength and support to see it through this difficult period? Or will this balancing act of having a competent Government and keeping Independence to the fore for its activists, founder on the rock of a Westminster inspired cash crisis and a chaotic Brexit offering an uncertain timescale? One thing is clear, the SNP will have to reach out to a wider and more diverse electorate. After a decade of power at Holyrood achieved by a broad-based populism, charismatic leadership, competent government, disciplined organisation and helped by the excesses of Westminster, nearly 50 per cent of Scots remain unimpressed or uninspired by the idea of leaving the UK. A hard Brexit could change this. Or are the seeds of a medium to longer term decline of the SNP already sown?

Political development in Scotland, post-devolution, has taken a different path from England. The obvious differences are the rise of the SNP from the margins of Scottish politics to majority government, a more inclusive nationalism, a deepening sense of national identity, and the rise in popularity of independence. There are other aspects of Scottish politics which suggest something more significant is happening to help shape the destiny of a nation, which was, until 1999, in the eyes of Westminster, no more than just another administrative region of the UK. Devolution in the first Blair Government was fulfilling the legacy of John Smith; but there was no 'bigger vision' for four nation politics or for radical constitutional change. This was an opportunity missed. It should be remembered that, pre-1997, persuading a majority of the Labour party in Scotland that devolution was a good thing was a monumental task on its own! We remain part of the UK's unwritten constitution. Will Scotland recognise the importance of people as citizens and see the worth of adopting a written constitution?

We need to develop our multi-party system in Scotland and make the case for a more progressive politics based on further electoral reform, including Westminster, coalition governments, less tribalism and more cooperation, and some realignment of political parties, ideas and policies. Is the Conservative party a sustainable resurgent force in Scotland? Can we expect political and party realignment, north and south of the border, as a way of modernising our politics and the only way to counter English and Scottish nationalism?

My Personal Political Journey

Citizens United reflects my own personal political journey of 30 years in elected office – as Councillor, MP and MSP, Minister in London and Edinburgh, Scottish First Minister and then 15 years serving Scotland by writing, arguing and, in more recent times, agonising about the fortunes of the Labour party. After 45 years of membership I remain committed to the party as a progressive force with an optimism and belief that is, first, firmly rooted in my own experiences; my early life in a mining town, my passion for football and the sense of community if inspired, and of course my family, especially my grandparents, who were socialists, Christians and deeply involved in working class politics, mining and football. It is, secondly, rooted a loyalty not founded in the current state of the party, but in the knowledge that the enduring principles and mission behind social democracy or democratic socialism are the best route to a fairer, just and more equal society. The early years of the 21st century have only confirmed the wisdom and relevance of these ideas. Finally, the Labour party was created in 1900 to address a set of problems and issues which, although different in context and appearance, remain very similar today and in many respects have become more challenging. The excesses of globalisation, austerity economics, neoliberalism, right wing populism and the relentless inroads of market principles into our social and public realms, merely confirm capitalism has not been tamed or effectively managed. People are suffering. They are angry, registering their disquiet and disillusion with traditional political parties and establishment elites in a variety of ways. People's feelings of betrayal, broken promises and lack of trust are screaming at us from every possible direction. People are aware of the shallowness of our democracy. People understand what broken politics is about. People know why there is a breakdown of trust between themselves and politicians. People want to be more than just a cross on a ballot paper every three or four years. This being the case, why have the traditional parties not woken up to their concerns? This is the task of all progressive parties, especially Labour.

But parties and politics must change. Believing in the principles, values, philosophy, and creed of one party shouldn't blind me or anyone else to the contributions other parties can make, or the fact that no party has the answer to every problem, or that each party's manifesto contains a unique accumulated wisdom of all the years, or even that people think in total absolutes on every subject. Life is more complicated than this and deserves to be respected. Fighting for the creed and values of a party may become more important than the parties themselves, if we are to embrace new ways of thinking and put common good ideas and collaboration before damaging and corrosive ideology and conflict. Our politics is hopelessly preoccupied with tribalism and intolerance.

There are also questions to be asked about much of the relevance of our political parties and their utility in a society which is undergoing such a transformation. Our politics should not only understand what is happening but, to confront and contest market excesses, the destructive nature of increasingly unfettered capitalism, the aggressive intrusion of market principles into every aspect of society and the relentless rise of inequality and its impact on the distribution of income, wealth, and opportunity.

Trump, Brexit, populism, and the rise of the right in European democracies, speak volumes about the fragile state of our politics and governance and the nature of our democracy and electorate. Trump and Brexit are not causes, but consequences of the deep seated anger, anxieties and sense of betrayal people feel about their lives, their place in society and their growing sense of being excluded and ignored. An overwhelming sense of bitterness and hate for those they believe to be responsible for their plight and a desire to reach out and embrace those who empathise with them and who appear to be listening. The election of Trump and the triumph of Brexit share a common electorate. Social, educational and economic factors help identify this rapidly growing group of voters and provides some explanation of this powerful anti-establishment, anti-elite group and the much talked about notion of the anti-expert that is now so evident in our politics and elections.

But there is a deeper crisis. We would be well advised to acknowledge that a vacuum has been created and politics and traditional parties must take responsibility for the turmoil that has engulfed western democracies. Large swathes of voters have had enough. Stagnant living standards, poor or declining wages, cuts in services, deepening inequality and the unfair distribution of income, wealth and opportunities are creating deep fractures in our society and a profound sense of grievance. The decline of social democracy in the last 30 years and its fading appeal to those who are being locked out of social and economic benefits, anger about austerity and the failure of the political classes to either acknowledge or respond to this crisis have cleared the path for the populists, extremists such as Le Pen, Farage, Wilders and Trump. Forget about all of this offending our elite sensibilities, our political decencies and middle class sensitivities. Forget about the coarsening of the political discourse and how unreasonable this has become. Forget the fact that the authoritarian populists bend, ignore or destroy the rules of political engagement. Focus instead on the fact that millions of people voted for them and that there is something rotten at the heart of our politics that requires urgent attention and remedy. Brexit is an example of how shallow leadership and a weak democracy can be ruthlessly exploited by zealots, fanatics and cheap political patriots to achieve a political outcome that bears no relation to the needs of Britain, Europe, or indeed, of many of those who voted Leave.

3

Brexit, a Cause Without a Case.
Why Did It Happen?

BREXIT IS THE result of complex and interrelated factors which ultimately came together, like a unique constellation of planets, and pushed voters in the UK/Britain to vote, by a slim margin, to leave the EU. Ranking with Suez and Iraq as one of the worst foreign policy blunders in the post-war period, Brexit is a spectacular reminder of the political and constitutional chaos Britain is about to enter. The significance of the EU campaign and its consequences cannot be overstated. It is a reminder of the risks facing our politics and our democracy. Poor governance, broken politics, treacherous and delusional behaviour in the form of the cheap patriots of the right of the Conservative party and a lack of any constitutional safeguards are driving a divided Britain to the edge and again casting doubt on Scotland's continued membership of the UK. Post-Brexit Westminster is light years away from four nation governance or any form of federalism or home rule or even abandoning the archaic idea of absolute Westminster sovereignty.

Very much a reflection of our declining union, weakening democracy and broken politics, the outcome of the EU referendum, has also laid bare any sense of national unity, purpose, or solidarity. Britain is tearing itself apart over a cause without a case, a national exercise in self-harm. To unravel how we find ourselves in such a catastrophic mess and why we need to escape from this madness, we need to look at a number of issues that are woven into the narrative, including:

- The extreme right in British politics, especially in the Conservative party.

- The Rust Belt analysis, Trump and Brexit and the backlash.
- Populism, old discredited ideas in a new garb.
- The myth of the absolute sovereignty of Westminster/supremacy of law.
- Sentiment, nostalgia, emotion, and the lure of greatness idea (more English Exit that British Brexit).
- Lies, distortions, and fake news.
- What's the matter with social democracy?
- The US, our friend and saviour.

The outcome of the EU referendum was a commentary on the state of Britain, not the EU or our membership of this highly successful institution, celebrating its 60th birthday and still a work in progress. This raises a key question, also the title of Thomas Frank's 2004 *New York Times* Best Seller book *What's the Matter with Britain?*. The narrow majority for leaving the EU, which has divided Britain even further, does not confirm that this is the settled will of the people. Voting for a sealed box makes no sense without knowing the contents, unless you are of a mind that you unconditionally despise the EU and are unmoved by any consequences that might follow. The mere fact of leaving the EU becomes the supreme outcome, a triumph in its own right. This is an absurd state of affairs. Surely the EU referendum result cannot be the last word on this epoch-making decision.

The political logic of this means that over the next two years the House of Commons, in partnership with the legislatures in Belfast, Cardiff and Edinburgh, derail the paving legislation – the seven Bills now before Parliament. There is a natural majority at Westminster for remaining in the EU. Progressive alliances at Westminster also have the option to reject the outcome of the EU negotiations in Brussels. In this scenario, the economic, social and political consequences of a hard Brexit are thrown out and we remain members of the Single Market and the Customs Union. This would effectively mean retaining membership of the EU. Depending on what evolves over the next few years, some or all of this could be put to the people in a referendum, or by a vote in Westminster and the other national legislatures, or all of the above.

This is a battle for Britain and to win the EU back. There is no doubt that there are countless permutations to consider in what is the most important decision facing us since 1945, but it seems inconceivable that we walk away from the present crisis and allow the right wing of the

Conservative party to do our country what they have been doing to their party.

The Rust Belt Analysis, Trump and Brexit

To understand Brexit, Trump and right wing populism, look no further than Naomi Klein's new book, *No is Not Enough* and Thomas Frank's *What's the Matter with Kansas?*, which reads like it was written yesterday. The books describe and explain what lies at the heart of some of the biggest political upheavals in post-war western democracies. This section of *Citizens United* sets out in stark and unapologetic terms the dangerous and divisive nature of Trump and Brexit, and similar developments in Europe, bringing to the fore again the discredited ideas which pose a real threat to our politics, democracy, and governance.

The US, the EU and the UK are in the grip of right wing populism, a threatening set of 'isms' and a virulent strain of economic nationalism which has echoed down through the post-war years.

Trump's campaign was emboldened by Brexit. These catastrophic victories have excited and enthused the right and far right in many European countries. The similarities of the Trump and Brexit campaigns are striking. Their shared aspirations, dislikes and political tactics are not a coincidence. Their political language may offend sensibilities and sensitivities, but no one should be in any doubt about what we are dealing with: these are people with serious intent to wreck much of what has been achieved in the last 80 years.

Contempt for the EU is the barely concealed desire on the part of the right in the US and Britain. Their fear of regional trade blocs, increasingly the norm in the globalised world of today, fuels their economic nationalism and reinforces their desire for unfettered free trade to make the US and Britain 'great' again. The free marketeers' ideology that politics should never get in the way of economics sits well with their notions of small government, small state involvement, low taxes, low welfare and ever greater access for market capitalism into the whole social and public realm. Extreme Brexiteers place their faith in the US as a saviour in a new Anglosphere. But in reality, these kindred spirits look set to ruin their respective countries, all in the name of the market.

This is not where Britain should be, but leaving the EU is, in astronomy terms, black hole territory where anything is possible.

On its publication in 2004, Thomas Frank's *What's the Matter with Kansas?* predicted the arrival of a Trump-like figure in the US. He based this conclusion on his analysis of the rising number of people in the state who had lost their faith in the American dream. Frank anticipated a backlash of anger, fear and resentment involving millions of people across the US, their alienation reinforced by the perception that they were being betrayed by the Democrats, and that the Republicans were not interested in working people and couldn't be trusted. Frank's argument was prescient, but by 2016, after a further 12 years of globalisation, technological change, austerity and automation, the arrival of a Trump repeated a now familiar pattern of events in post-war democracies, in a process involving the following elements:

- Neoliberal austerity, the growth of cultural identity and a souring of the public mood against elites and experts perceived to buttress the status quo with little sympathy or respect for working people.
- The intrusion of the market into public, political and social realms.
- Cultural anger hijacked to achieve economic ends for the exploiters.
- Religious intolerance, xenophobia and nativism prominent in the debate.
- The 'Rust Belt' syndrome of anger, pain and disillusionment with social democracy at the fore.
- An intense desire to ascribe blame whether accurately or not.

In this context, the certainties of life have disappeared for many people. With the present trashed and few dreams to look forward to, nostalgia of the past kicks in. Even in the realisation that nothing might be on offer from either Brexit or Trump, people in their millions voted as a statement of protest.

Trump, the brand and businessman, shares the view with the right of the Conservative party that countries should be run like companies in which the market substitutes for democracy, wealth is worth, greed is good and people service money instead of the other way around. Trump has taken matters further by turning the White House into another piece of real estate in which all the family and business interests can prosper. He is the head of his own parallel universe. Business as usual. The more he veers from the 'normal', the more his base is drawn to him. Public truths are being obliterated and he has his own truths and alternative facts.

Trump pretends he is the enemy of elites and presents himself as the voice of downtrodden and forgotten Americans, claims that as a consummate deal maker and job creator he is capable of fixing the broken economic system. A self-styled Twitter expert, he uses social media to speak directly to his base, constantly denigrating the 'fake news' spread by the mainstream media. (Whereas, for hard Brexiteers, a predominantly anti-EU press in the UK obviates the need for an alternative communications channel.)

For over 40 years, dominant UK press attitudes towards the EU, ranging from ambivalence to hostility, have starved people of balanced views on Europe. This was fake news, rampant before the term was even coined, has been severely damaging to the European cause. It is hard to escape the conclusion that Britain is in such a mess now because of a fake referendum.

The Extreme Right in British Conservative Politics

The Conservative party has had a civil war raging for a generation and this has now spilled over. Not content with nearly destroying their own party, they are using Britain as a new battleground. They promulgate the nonsense that the mere act of leaving the EU will solve every problem? Brexit represents a completely pointless exercise, a waste of valuable time, resources and energy. Rather than undergoing a wonderful transformation, Britain is tearing itself apart.

The hard Brexiteers on the right of the Conservative party are the true enemy within. Destroying Britain seems far too high a price to pay for allowing this group to wreak havoc as part of a wider assault on Britain and its way of life. The Tories have form on this issue. David Cameron and John Major both saw their careers destroyed by the hard right euro-cynics and it seems likely that Theresa May will soon join them. For the hard-liners, leaving the EU is only the first stage in their mission to push Britain towards isolationism. Bilateral trade deals with other economic nationalists, cutting back government, diminishing the role of the state and allowing the market to undermine our democracy will reinforce neoliberal austerity measures for the many and continue the feather-bedding of the few. Removing Britain from the protectionist clutches of an intervening Brussels bureaucracy is the first, but absolutely vital step in changing Britain.

Their narrative is recreating the idea of the Anglosphere, including the special relationship with the US. They see the US as more than a special friend, market believer and home of individualism: the see it as our saviour. The arrival of Trump has emboldened the right of the Conservative party, who see his presidency helping to create Britain in the image of the US. What a troubling thought.

A hard Brexit, out of the Single Market and the Customs Union, would force the Conservative government to give substance to this idea of an offshore bargain basement Britain. The idea of a special relationship, now past its sell by date as far as most diplomats are concerned, is laughable, but the 'no deal is better than a bad deal' mantra could push Britain that way.

The destruction by fire of Grenfell Tower in London illustrates the potential outcome of regulations contrived not to upset the so-called freedom of the market. The Tory right hates regulations and they are obsessed about removing them and minimising their application. This lies behind their commitment to cutting back big government. Regulations run counter to their market philosophy, add costs the market doesn't want to bear and create more bureaucracy – from this perspective, one of the reasons why the EU must go.

Protecting Britain in times of Tory Governments has been one of the benefits of the EU. There should be real concern about the EU Repeal Bill now before the House of Commons, as some of the vital social, environmental and employment protections may not be incorporated into British Law.

Looked at in isolation, leaving the EU is problematic enough, but when you consider the real agenda of the Conservative party there is a great deal more to worry about. Would the same Leave result be obtained if the simple binary question was postscripted with the statement that, on leaving, we will move towards more market, more commercialisation of our social and public realms, the scrapping of thousands of regulations, a removal of social and employment laws, less government, more economic nationalism and isolationism, and closer links with the US, Turkey, the Philippines and Saudi Arabia. If so, the result might well have been different.

The present political chaos within the Conservative party and their shambolic handling of Brexit leads to the conclusion that Britain would be a better place without either.

What's the Matter with Social Democracy?

Understanding fully why Brexit happened, allows us to make a stronger case for the UK to remain in the EU. The Brexit campaign was passionate, vocal and visible, and unconstrained by the facts about what the EU has actually been doing in the 60 years of its existence. The daily megaphone cheerleading from partisan newspapers was wholly destructive of balanced debate. At best, an ounce of half-truth was accompanied by a ton of lies, distortions and pure fantasy.

This raises the question of the Labour leadership during the EU campaign. There seems to be no doubt that if Labour had mounted a half decent campaign, Remain would have won. A leadership still clinging to old ideas of the EU and echoing some of the doubts of the early post-war period went AWOL for most of the campaign. The rest is history. Labour voters, confused about the party's message, were swayed by anti-EU rhetoric from other sources who had been preparing for this campaign since we became members in 1972. This point is only of significance in terms of the future.

To save Britain from a catastrophic future, the Labour party should now change course and make amends to the British people by fully committing to remaining in the EU and building a progressive alliance with other parties, including the sane element of the Conservative party. This is what democracy means.

Jeremy Corbyn has said he respects the decision to leave. That doesn't mean that others have to accept or agree with it. Labour is an internationalist party with strong links to the left in Europe, where trades unionists want Britain to remain in the EU. Young people see their future in the EU.

Britain is Changing

Public opinion is changing. People are asking, what are the benefits to be gained in leaving the EU? Some have decided that Brexit is a mistake after all. We are witnessing preparations for Brexit that are evidently shambolic, made by a Government that lacks any clarity, direction or real understanding of what is at stake. Progressives in both the US and Europe think that Britain has taken leave of its senses.

Theresa May is supposedly reaching out to the other parties for help in her time of need. She deserves no help. It is her party that has created this mess. The die is not cast. People must not allow themselves to be browbeaten into thinking that nothing can be done.

The Tory Brexiteers feel secure because of the failure of their leadership to evict them. They are running amok, bankrolled by a network of rich backers who share the same deranged policies. Brexit has been, to date, their greatest success.

If this spirit of invincibility is to be crushed, then remaining in the EU would be a significant start in ousting those who are taking advantage of broken politics, a declining union, a very weak democracy and a dysfunctional system of governance that is not fit for purpose. If you throw into this mix the decline of liberalism, socialism and social democracy, not only here but throughout western democracies, the struggle to Remain can be seen as part of a much bigger effort to halt the march of economic nationalism, authoritarianism and isolationism. We need to out the right of the Conservative party and expose the real damage they are inflicting on this country.

Dealing with Democracy

If we are to remain in the EU, we have to deal effectively with democratic reality of the vote that created a narrow margin for Britain to leave the EU. There is no doubt that we have to acknowledge and respect the integrity and sincerity of the people who wanted to leave at a moment in time, based on a set of conditions and knowledge. That vote reflected their reality. There should however, be a way of moving that debate forward. When Brexit is given its actual meaning and substance, the wider fraud will be exposed as the biggest mistake in Britain's post-war history; genuine concerns have been comprehensively exploited. Then the British people should be entitled to a new chance to decide.

There is no serious reason for a defeated party in any vote or referendum to just walk away. Recent experience of the EU and Scottish referendums have shown how bitter, divisive and unforgiving they can be. Referendums are a dangerous political weapon where the outcome of a massively complex issues is reduced to a binary choice. This unfortunately creates binary mindsets. There is no written constitution to guide us and we are left to the whims of a Westminster government and parliament to decide when a referendum is to be deployed.

Much of the rhetoric surrounding referendums is couched in terms of informed choice. Even accepting the most generous interpretation of that, you would be hard placed to say that the EU referendum satisfied the criteria. This issue highlights wider questions about our democracy and raises doubts about how the UK could take such an enormous decision in the most ill-informed and divisive manner, on a whole range of issues which have more to do with the condition and mindset of Britain today, rather than any relevance to the EU. Never in the field of political endeavour has so much vitriol and abuse been hurled at one institution by so few with such potential catastrophic consequences for the many. Brexit is about the state of Britain, not the EU.

Absolute Sovereignty and the Primacy of Our Laws

In a world of interdependence, internationalism and global interconnectedness, absolute sovereignty as a concept has little meaning. This idea has figured prominently in the EU referendum and in subsequent debates, with the clear inference that if we could only remove ourselves from the EU, we would get our sovereignty back and everything would fall into place. Britain could be great again. We would have our country back. We would make our laws again.

Where has the country been since 1972?

What does absolute sovereignty really mean?

For centuries, Westminster has believed in the idea of absolute sovereignty of the institution and has repelled any notion that this is not a secure idea. There are significant implications for our politics, democracy and governance. In the absence of any written constitution, this has allowed Westminster, supported by both major parties, to argue that nothing in Britain happens without their expressed agreement; while they might cede some authority, devolve some decision-making to the nations of the UK, they will never give power away or share power. Notwithstanding the political outcry this might create, Westminster, with a one-line Bill, could abolish the Scottish Parliament tomorrow and take all the powers back to Westminster. This is unlikely to happen, but it could. From the world outside the Westminster bubble, it seems ludicrous that they would want to hang on to an outdated idea that clashes with the Realpolitik of the 21st century. And while absolute sovereignty means absolute power over everything, a quick survey of the political world we live in would show sovereignty, in its purest form, to be a redundant idea and a major obstacle to success in the more progressive environment of the EU and western democracies.

Germany, a more powerful and more successful country than the UK, with a world-class leader in Angela Merkel, seems to cope with sharing sovereignty and aspirations with 27 other nation states. Why does Britain have this unique condition among social democracies? Does absolute sovereignty have more to do with where Britain has been in the past rather than where it is going in the future?

Because Britain is run without a written constitution, Westminster can virtually make it up as it goes along, with no competing power base. This is one of the reasons why some of the fanatics resent Brussels. In every other country in the EU, a written constitution means power to the people, not to politicians. Even in the US, Congress does not have absolute sovereignty and works by diktat of the constitution with the president, the Supreme Court and the 50 States. There is no reason why the parliamentary system in Britain should continue to operate in such a medieval manner, sanctifying the exclusive politics of Westminster. When people were being fed with the notion that they needed to win their country back, this was all about Westminster, not them.

Absolute sovereignty is a plaything of the political classes at Westminster and, in particular, the right of the Conservative party. Dressed up as the saviour of the national interest with a pride of Britain sentiment, this concept has stirred the hearts and history of people. But if Brexit ever becomes a reality, it will mean absolutely nothing to the millions of people who voted Leave.

Staying with the myth of absolute sovereignty, a particularly virulent strain of paranoia has been aimed at the European Court of Justice (ECJ). Theresa May seems obsessed with making sure Britain has no links with the ECJ. This piece of fanaticism is linked to the supremacy of British Law. Once again this is reminiscent of the partisan war chants at Westminster after the 2014 Scottish Independence referendum where David Cameron led the charge on English votes for English Laws. The ECJ only rules on strictly EU matters in the form of regulations, directions and, importantly, the treaties upon which everything and anything that happens in the EU, must be based. These treaties, are unanimously agreed by all 28 member states, including Britain. It also plays an important role in the operation of the Single Market, especially in relation to the four fundamental freedoms of people, goods, services and finance.

The House of Commons Library, one of the most impressive and objective institutions of research, has confirmed that about 18 per cent of our legislation comes from Europe. So where is the problem?

The European Courts

Another institution that irks the fanatical is the European Court of Human Rights (ECHR). Based in Strasbourg, the ECHR oversees the work of the European Convention of Human Rights and has played a remarkably successful role in the vital area of upholding human rights; the 47 countries represented on the Council of Europe now lead the world in this whole exercise of looking after each other. Created by the Council of Europe in the early post-war years, both the Convention and the Court were amongst the inspirational ideas of Sir Winston Churchill who played a leading role in their formative years.

For the predatory Tory right, once they succeed in junking the European Court of Justice, who or what is their next target? Might it be the ECHR? Why not? If the isolationists get their farcical way, why not remove ourselves from the International Court of Justice and the International Criminal Court? And why stop there? Trump doesn't like the UN for the same reasons the right of the Conservative party here objects to foreign aid, immigration and the flight of refugees to Britain. Our membership of the Security Council may be a block on that. So, like Trump, do we have a problem with the North Atlantic Treaty Organisation (NATO), especially when so many countries in his eyes are dragging their feet in terms of achieving the 2 per cent expenditure on defence?

Sharing sovereignty is the most natural thing in an interconnected world. It would be absurd for Britain to dismantle our global interests, diminishing ourselves as the victim of the delusional at the expense of our European allies who, despite our odd behaviour, want to be close.

There is no absolute sovereignty in a world of interdependence. It makes sense to share our aspirations, spread our risks and partner up to tackle opportunities. Brexiteers seem to think that this is a worthwhile strategy, as long as the EU, especially the ECJ, is excluded. But pursuing economic and political nationalism is the antithesis of any notion of making Britain great again.

At the heart of this is the lack of a written constitution. This allows successive British Governments to act like 'elected dictatorships', with no checks or balances. Our politics, governance and democracy are shaped in the image of a Government at Westminster that will not cede power and pays only lip service to the opposition parties or the national parliaments and assemblies of the UK.

The Lies, Fake and Fraudulent News

People are alive to the fact that politicians, elites, experts and the establishment can be economical with the truth and often egg the pudding to gain some advantage or sell a story or idea. However, the EU referendum campaign descended to spectacular depths in terms of deceit and distortion on an industrial scale, deceit.

Despite our membership of the European Economic Community (EEC), the European Commission (EC) and now the EU, dating from 1972, there has never been a European golden age where any EU business has been given positive coverage by the right leaning press, which has provided a litany of trivia, exaggeration and prolonged and consistent denigration of anything to do with Europe, the ECHR or the ECJ. With so many in their ranks at best ambivalent and unwilling to give credit for the benefits Britain has received, the political classes have allowed an anti-Europe culture to emerge.

For 45 years the EU was portrayed as the enemy of Britain, so it is little wonder that the EU became a friend we didn't get to know. It paints a picture of Euro neglect where successive British Governments, never good team players, allowed nearly 50 years of EU vitriol and poison to pass without any serious opposition.

Law Making

'We need to make our own laws and not be run by Brussels' has been the war cry of much of the Brexit assault on the EU, with the Brussels bureaucrats getting the blame for running and ruining our lives.

This very much smacks of the 'English votes for English laws' David Cameron was so enthusiastic about after the Scottish Independence referendum. The UK parliament has not stopped making laws. Every piece of legislation passed in Brussels has to conform to the purpose and intent of the various EU treaties that govern every action of the EU. Every treaty has to be unanimously agreed by every member state. Listening to Brexiteers, you would be forgiven for thinking that foreigners are lining up day after day to legislate against Britain's national interests, with us nowhere to be seen. Not true. The European Parliament has no power to initiate legislation, which makes it one of the weakest parliaments among western democracies. This was the deliberate intention of each member state, including Britain. One of the main criticisms of the EU is that it is undemocratic. Yes, that is true but this situation reflects the conscious will of all the member states to keep it in that condition. That hasn't prevented the Brexiteers hypocritically criticising the EU for being undemocratic when responsibility lies with the member states not the EU.

Legislation, mainly regulations and directives, is created by the European Commission, with UK representation and the Council of Ministers, again representing the 28 member states. The European Parliament will then start the legislative process and, of course, there is a massive presence of British MEPs representing our interests. There is a European Council overseeing the strategic direction of all of this, where again the Prime Minister participates. Finally, there is oversight from the ECJ, again involving British judges. This may seem like an elaborate bureaucracy, but this is what successive British Governments have participated in and agreed to, at the same time having denied any real democratisation of the process. The long-term ambivalence and at times indifference to the European project by successive British governments has, by default, allowed few reforms to take place. It is worth noting that as far as law making is concerned, the EU Parliament is weak and heavily shackled by Member States.

The EU is the product of its members, something conveniently forgotten by British governments. Other governments have helped shape these institutions, but Britain has never been at the centre of any serious attempt at reform, and has instead shouted from the sidelines; we have accepted membership without taking any real responsibility and created the conditions for the crisis that is Brexit.

Immigration and Borders

Regaining control of our borders became a powerful mantra during the EU campaign. For the sake of accuracy, it must be said that Britain has never lost control of its borders. The lack of a coherent and strategic immigration policy and borders strategy is a completely different matter and has more to do with British inertia than with the EU.

What those who supported Leave seem to be against is the free movement of European people, which forms one of the four key themes of the Single Market. Margaret Thatcher was at least was honest about her embrace of the unfettered free market, the current right wing of the Conservative party is content to link many of our national problems with EU migrants and also to 'out' them. In the referendum immigration was exploited. The genuine concerns of the many were used for the benefit of the political and personal ambitions of a few on the right of the Conservative party.

Of probably more significance was the decision of Prime Minister Blair to waive the offer of a seven-year transition for new migrants from the EU after the accession of eight Eastern European countries in 2004. The subsequent period of rapid growth in the number of EU nationals coming to the UK has undoubtedly made managing this number of people much more difficult. Again, this problem was made in Britain.

But again, the right wing blitz against migrants and open borders misses the fact that we are not members of the Schengen agreement providing for open borders. We do control our borders. What Britain does with its borders is not decided in Brussels. Once again, the weakness of Britain – our inability to spend because of austerity, the cuts in the workforce and our general incompetence – is being blamed on Europe at a time when half of Britain's inward migration is non-European.

Opt-outs

Schengen is one of the four opt-outs from the EU negotiated by previous British Governments, information sank without trace in the campaign. Britain has more opt-outs that any other country in the EU, once again contradicting the widely held view that Brussels bulldozes us into everything.

In addition to Schengen we have three other opt-outs: membership of the eurozone, Justice and Security (where we pick and choose) and the Charter of Fundamental Rights. These opt-outs show the extent to which flexibility does exist to secure national interests, a fact of which most people have no idea – which of course fits the much pedalled impression of the EU as the tyrannical inflexible ogre doing us down at every turn.

The Trade Myth

The saying goes that you can judge a person or party by the company they keep. The Conservative party's enthusiasm for economic nationalism and their 'make Britain great again after we win our country back' slogan has seen Ministers and the Prime Minister cosying up and selling their wares to economic hard men such as Trump, Recep Tayyip Erdogan of Turkey, Duterte of the Philippines and the Saudis. Illustrating the desperate plight of what comes next after leaving the EU, the Government seems eager to impress, regardless of human rights, climate change and other important considerations. We are seeking comfort with other economic nationalists and taking big risks with Britain's future.

The uncertain world that Theresa May wants to be part of puts Britain at the mercy of bilateral trade and basic World Trade Organisation (WTO) conditions. It means losing the security of the largest single market in the world, giving up on being the top trading regional bloc in the world after China, absorbing tariff increases with the EU and being exposed to the hostile trading climate outside the Single Market.

What is Britain's reward in all of this self-inflicted pain? Has the Conservative party identified one single trade benefit from Brexit? President Trump, our new best friend equates world trade with the casino operations in his hotels, where outcomes are unpredictable, but still provide much fun. He wants to run the US as a company, which is the impression you also get from Theresa May about Britain. Both believe in unfettered markets. It is incomprehensible that anyone can invest trust in the unpredictable Trump or fail to see that his America First line relegates every other trading partner to second place. This is not the company we want to keep. There is no prospect of recreating a new Anglosphere. A misplaced, sentimentalised sense of history may yet become the rock on which we perish.

It is complete madness to suggest that membership of the Customs Union and the Single Market are holding us back, or that escaping from the jurisdiction of the ECJ will free us from a judicial tyranny.

Only recently, the EU completed the first stage of a deal with Japan and completed a deal with Canada. Although the trade deal with the US has, for now, failed, there were hopes of if it being recast and further developed. Trump has ensured that this is unlikely to happen. The US president is unhappy with the North American Free Trade Agreement (NAFTA), a trade deal that involves Canada, Mexico and the US, and has withdrawn from the new trading bloc being established in the Asia Pacific region. Trump is unreliable and unpredictable. He has diminished the US in the eyes of the world, handed a new leadership role to China after they seem likely to take over the US's role in Asian trade agreement and has passed the mantle of the leader of the free world to German Chancellor Merkel, after his crazed remarks about NATO and the EU. Again, you cannot escape the obvious conclusion that the Tory right are trying to dictate the destiny of the UK. In place of a secure, stable, and predictable trade arrangements within the EU, extremists want to exchange certainty with the uncertainty and swear allegiance to economic nationalism, the delusional benefits of unfettered market capitalism and Trump.

Despite the efforts of the Brexiteers to obscure the timescale for this new trading paradise to emerge, very few deals will become a reality in the timescales being predicted. Trade negotiations take a very, very long time. The WTO operates at a snail's pace because trade issues are so complex and despite Trump's enthusiasm a trade deal with the US could take up to a decade to achieve.

The lack of honest and transparency on trade suggests that the Tories haven't a clue as to what they are doing, or that they are keen to hide the realities from the public, or both. Trade is the life-blood of Britain and any interruption to current patterns of trade relationships and membership of the Single Market would be disastrous and diminish Britain as an economic force. Trade Secretary Liam Fox, on a recent visit to the WTO, blundered into saying that politics gets in the way of economics. Fox is a free marketeer whose stance would weaken our already fragile industrial base and undermine our ability to address the continuing challenges of globalisation, automation and technology against the background of austerity and deepening inequality.

Britain is on the cusp of a technological revolution in which profound labour market changes, robotics, Artificial Intelligence and communications will change the face of Britain for ever. Instead of being preoccupied with building a better future, the parliaments and assemblies in our four nations are dealing with the pointless distraction of Brexit.

In this broad sweep of trade issues, it is worth remembering we haven't touched on the challenges faced by the different sectors of business, commerce and industry, whose practical needs are very much intertwined with the EU. Immigration is a problem of Britain's own making. We have never had a sensible immigration strategy or policies and the genuine concerns of British people have been left unattended for decades. Tory MP, Enoch Powell gave us an insight into the politics of hate, race and colour a generation ago.

Trade isn't just about moving products from one place to another. The context for this is extremely challenging requiring well-crafted rules, regulations and laws which cover a remarkable range of technical details, safety regulations and consumer rights and much more. There is also the question of borders and customs, which currently don't exist for trade within the EU, but will soon be in place if we leave and have a hard Brexit. How will people deal with border crossings between Ireland and Northern Ireland? The history of this previously troubled part of the UK suggest this is another potential consequence of a bad idea.

Immigration and Trade

It seems a pity that Brexiteers have elevated and exploited immigration as their main weapon of choice. The poisonous impact on Britain has created bitter divisions. Acts of racism, religious intolerance and xenophobia have grown in the aftermath of the EU referendum. More lies have been told about immigration than on any other EU issue.

Leaving aside the wider implications of immigration, the scrapping of the free movement of people as part of leaving the Single Market lies at the heart of economic and trade issues. We need foreign workers for our construction and service industries, farming and NHS. We also need foreign students, technologists, scientists, researchers, educationalists, and countless others. This is how the modern world works and it is the same for the other 27 EU countries. We can't live outside reality. The consequences of turning immigration into the key Brexit issue are the responsibility of the right of British politics. There are concerns to be tackled, but once again a single destructive issue is blinding us to the benefits of an interconnected world, a sense of internationalism and a broader humanity. But we must also face up to the hard reality that successive governments have ignored genuine non-racial and non-religious concerns about the geographical impact of inward flows of migrants.

Confronting the Tories

The Labour party is trying to decide whether they should contest or coexist with the idea of leaving the Single Market. Too often the party's policies are very similar to the Tories.

Business is too conservative and reserved to speak up and slap down the ideologues who are behind this mayhem or to make waves against a Government it is sympathetic too.

The right leaning press are unwilling to criticise and are still championing the diminishing of Britain in the eyes of our allies, and seem silent on the damage that will be caused to our economy if a hard Brexit becomes a reality.

Broadcasters are too polite to comment on what is really happening and call it as it is. In their search for fair and balanced coverage, they invariably give too much weight to the plausible and the delusional.

The other parties at Westminster are up for a fight, but need Labour and the true patriots in the Conservative party to give a lead.

A vacuum has been created in which the natural enemies of Brexit remain unsure of the public mood. Although it is shifting against Brexit, they worry about how bold they can be. The burden of a referendum result weighing heavily on their minds, Labour MPs are concerned about a backlash from Brexit voters.

MPs at Westminster are enjoying the summer break of 2017 in the full knowledge that they will soon be back to a nightmare of seven Bills and a vote in September on the second reading of the Repeal Bill. For our legislators, nothing else of real substance or significance will interrupt this pointless exercise for two years. Brexit is casting a long shadow over our future and needs to be derailed, deconstructed and eventually destroyed. Remaining in the Single Market (and preferably the Customs

Union) will be key to unravelling Brexit. It will require acceptance of the free movement of people, a financial payment to the ongoing work of the EU and remaining within the jurisdiction of the ECJ.

Britain Not a Team Player

Setting aside the ideology of the right and the politics and psychology of the EU referendum campaign, it has to be asked: Why can't Britain be a good team player? Why can't Britain learn lessons from Germany? There, the social partnership model is yielding higher productivity, more investment in capital goods, giving morality a say alongside the market, offering serious protections for workers, priority for manufacturing, not just for financial services, and an industrial strategy. How novel. All of this achieved in a country comfortable with its membership of the EU and, horror of horrors, part of the eurozone. Why can Germany cope?

Britain has an attitude problem and its governance, constitution and politics are holding us back. Blaming all our ills on the EU and claiming that leaving would solve all our problems is a bit of a stretch. Evidence suggests the opposite. Our problems are made in Britain and we should stop 'outing' others for our weaknesses and deficiencies. The EU is not holding us back. We lack any sense of a progressive partnership mentality, there is an over-reliance on the market, a lack of national confidence in what we do, an absence of assuredness as to where we are in the world, and an emptiness of purpose and intent. We seem more content to find scapegoats rather than solutions for our current malaise. Our sense of future seems to be receding, but we can't keep embracing the past and call this progress.

The EU is the whipping boy for Britain's failures. Forensic scientists are not required, the evidence abounds. The right of British politics have created a tsunami of baseless ideas which washed over Britain in 2016. If these cheap patriots are left unchecked, what next for a struggling Britain or a UK in decline?

Leaving the EU is a defeat for Britain not a victory. It doesn't have to be like this.

4

Identity – Sentiment, Nostalgia, Emotion and the Lure of Greatness

IDENTITY IS COMPLEX political concept. People have multiple identities which cover every conceivable aspect of life. These can range from being a passionate football supporter devoted to one club, to a life-long member of a political party, to being proud of your country and a loyal patriot. The mind is an incredible repository of lived experiences, memories, real or imaginary, dreams and harsh realities generated by circumstances which change over time and can shape moods, generate feelings and influence behaviour, and totally frame how you live and how you think.

The 21st century has seen significant changes in politics which reflect the qualities, beliefs and shifting identities of voters and a move away from broad based politics to a much more focused way of registering likes and dislikes, and making statements of how people feel at different moments in time. The electorate is fragile, volatile and less influenced by the enduring thoughts of the two traditional parties in the UK and the US. They are now more influenced by nationality and economic conditions.

The fears, anger and pain that people experience often curdle into grudge, grievance and resentment politics: The most base part of this would have to be described as 'F*** You Politics!', derived from a sense of:

'We might not believe what's on offer, but we need to register our anger and despair as to what the future holds.'

The Trump and Brexit campaigns acted as a hook for concerns oft people feel that have been ignored.

Embracing the Past

Many people don't see a future for themselves and become trapped in nostalgia and the sense that better times have slipped away. This reflects the 'Rust Belt' phenomenon of the US and the UK and the backlash experienced in Brexit and the US presidential campaign. On the darker side, both campaigns allowed these cries for help to become caught up in a 'them and us' scenario where the plight of the left-behind is blamed on something or someone. This is where populism becomes ugly. Race, immigration, xenophobia, nativism and religious intolerance are a poisonous cocktail.

A shared sense of identity can create the basis of national cohesion and solidarity. The EU referendum campaign didn't have that feel about it, nor did the Scottish referendum held in 2014. Referendums are proving to be a remarkably divisive way of agreeing matters of public policy. While a sense of national identity in each of the four countries within the UK looks set to become more important, there seems little chance that a unity of shared purpose and ambition can be realised. It could be argued that identity has always driven politics, but the nature of this has changed dramatically. Britain's failure, up to now, to understand the complex dynamic of identity will lead to further constitutional upheaval, a diminishing sense of solidarity and security, and a declining sense of national purpose. Populism highlights the challenges of identity as it cuts through ideas of a simple class based analysis and seeks to shape our politics and democracy in different ways.

Sentiment and Emotion

The politics of nostalgia, sentiment and emotion – linked to identity and age – played an important role in Brexit. Vast numbers of Leave voters are real patriots, care about their country and are proud of Britain's past. Hard Brexiteers offered a false return to the triumphs of the past, with all Britain's lost grandeur and success, if only we could leave the EU, which was characterised as the great millstone around our necks, preventing us from being great again. This was designed to exploit the sincere emotions of millions of people. The emotional blackmail deployed by the hard Brexiteers is a statement about the failings of Britain, not the EU. Analysis of the EU referendum result suggests this was mainly an issue in England. This is a powerful and difficult issue to deal with. It would be easy to dismiss the lure of the past as nothing more than soft sentiment of the 'little Englander' mentality, that shouldn't be taken seriously. This would be a mistake.

Respect the People

For Labour, the dilemma is simple but challenging. First the referendum result was democratic, so, to use Jeremy Corbyn's words, we must 'respect the result'. That might suggest we don't need to agree with the result or accept it. Respect is the important point. Emotions were stirred up around a false prospectus. How do we address people's concerns while seeking to remain in the EU? How do we argue without arrogance or elitism that people's concerns have been abused by the right and other hard Brexiteers?

We need to have a strategy over the next two years to derail and ultimately destroy Brexit, while at the same time facing up to the pain people are experiencing and addressing their economic needs. In the US and the UK respectively, 63 million voted for Trump and 17.4 million voted to leave the EU. In Britain we need a much bigger and more inspired political strategy that starts to phase out the EU as the problem and instead focus on the real problem – the right wing of the Conservative party, austerity, market excesses and neoliberal economics, and Britain itself: this includes, 'those left behind'. Remaining in the EU must be part of a wider political campaign.

Britain seems to have given up talking about the future. This plays in to the game plan of those who want to evoke memories of the past and exploit them. The majority of people who voted Leave are, unlike the Tory right and other hard Brexiteers, not racists or xenophobes or economic nationalists. They are real patriots who need a vision to call their own and a future for their families; they need to feel part of a positive movement that looks forward to better economic times ahead.

The present time offers an opportunity for Brexit and populism to be defeated. Labour must recognise that patriotism and identity politics are a challenge, not a threat.

We might mock, 'winning our country back' and 'making Britain great again', but why is it that progressive parties in Britain have allowed such sentiments to gain such currency? This is a wake-up call for the political left who dismiss identity politics as a distraction from class politics. People need a sense of now, a sense of future and less need to dig into their past for comfort and security. Britain is a country with more memories than dreams. What is the British dream?

Trump and the hard Brexiteers made a great deal of economic arguments. Both offered great deals but nothing will be delivered. Their politics ensure that their priorities are elsewhere.

This raises the important question of why people can be persuaded to vote against their own economic interests by the political right. Trump made offered the 'left-behinds' a new deal. After his victory, he promised to slash corporation taxes, cut income tax for the wealthy, deregulate Wall Street, regardless of the 2008 crisis, and filled his cabinet with billionaires and multi-millionaires. In addition, if his efforts to replace Obamacare with Trumpcare succeed, another 20 million people will have no health care insurance. Most of them voted for Trump.

This parallels the situation in Britain. Brexit is an illusion, a fraud that will not benefit working people and will only hasten the day when more aggressive free market policies widen inequalities and put ideology first.

Social Democrats, Liberals and Socialists have created a vacuum in Britain and the US, and in many countries in Western Europe, which has been filled by populism, the rise of the right and the hollowing out of our public and social realms. Trump and the hard Brexiteers are beneficiaries of the lack of a public narrative or philosophy which offers an alternative to the madness which is unfolding in the US and the UK.

5

Populism: Discredited Ideas in New Garb

WHAT IS THE populist radical right? They are in most countries in Europe and are in the ascendency in the US and Britain as Trump and Brexit lead the way in overturning settled ways of running democracies and satisfying political demands. Although manifestations vary from country to country, populism brings together diverse national histories, a range of ideologies and different political strategies. There are, however, core concerns on the radical right that are easily identified. In a paper published by the Policy Network entitled 'Populist Euroscepticism and British Politics', four key elements are identified:

- Ethnic nationalism – a desire for the nation state to be sovereign and to protect the national culture and identity from 'alien' forces.
- Authoritarianism – an emphasis on maintaining the social order, by providing strong powers to traditional authorities such as the police and pursuing harsh policies against criminals and terrorists who threaten social order.
- Xenophobia – an often irrational and emotive hostility to foreigners, and to native minorities such as Muslims who are perceived as threatening others.
- Populism in the form of disaffection from mainstream politics and hostility to mainstream political elites who are regarded as ignoring the interests of, 'the people'.

At the base of Brexit these core concerns are obvious, along with other signature trademarks mentioned in earlier chapters.

EU *Becomes the Problem*

Over the past decade, the Policy Networks argues that it has become much easier for the populists to argue that Europe is 'the problem' as:

- The source of immigration threatening British jobs and cultural identity.
- The source of judicial rulings protecting terrorists and criminals who threaten British safety.
- The source of a corrupt and self-serving elite political culture.
- The source of endless rules and legislation limiting British Sovereignty and threatening British identity.

Reinforcing the themes of this book, the Policy Network says:

the party (Conservative) must find a way to balance the tension between two very different constituencies – of mainstream right wing, often libertarian, Eurosceptics, and of populist, authoritarian radical right wingers.

Despite suffering recent set-backs, populism remains a powerful force in France, Denmark, Austria, Switzerland, Norway, Netherlands, Germany, Italy and Britain. Populist parties of the left and centre left have also arisen in Europe, including Podemos in Spain and Syriza in Greece.

Dealing with populism is difficult because it is not a neat ideology but more a political logic, a way of thinking about problems. It is not bounded by class and, despite the hypocrisy of people like former UKIP leader Farage and Foreign Secretary Boris Johnston, they are able to call out their opponents as self-serving and undemocratic elites.

Right wing populists champion the people against elites who they accuse of pandering to and supporting a third group, such as immigrants. In the US and Britain, they can take on the business community, which most Conservatives have difficulty doing. Just as there is no common ideology that defines populism, there is not one constituency of the people. Similarly, there is no common identification of what the 'establishment' is. This makes the politics of populism difficult to comprehend and fight against.

US *Populism*

People who felt excluded are warming to spivs and charlatans, leaving behind people and parties that seemed to have been on their side for many decades. Populism thrives on discontent and grievance and the phenomenon that, once people have freed themselves from traditional voting patterns, they become emboldened and unpredictable.

The US has a history of populism which has often been a product of the politics of the southern states, where race, poverty and white supremacy have boosted to the far right. This has not been the case in the UK. Here, populism in its most virulent form arrived with UKIP. Extremists such as the British National Party (BNP) were minor fringe parties, never widely popular and largely ignored by a decent voting public.

The Conservative party is now more complex. Populists, in the shape of hard Brexiteers and the extreme right, drive a market agenda but are now too easily tempted by xenophobia cloaked in moderate language and plausible arguments, but unmistakably intolerant. One thing is clear: the progressive parties have a mountain to climb, because populism and the rise of the right have a serious grip on the current direction Britain is moving in.

The US *As Our Friend and Saviour*

An unstable president is not the answer to Britain's problem, either inside or outside the EU. It is quite unnerving to see Britain seeking to break bread with such a misguided economic nationalist, a climate change denier and xenophobe.

After celebrating 60 years of success, the EU is aware of the need for change, probably radical change. Earlier this year the EU issued a consultative paper outlining five scenarios for the future of the institution. There is wide spread recognition that the EU cannot continue without significant reform if it is to secure the commitment of the other 27 countries and start to deal with the big issues of climate change, austerity, inward migration and the strengthening of all the economies of member states, including those in the eurozone. Ambivalence over the last 45 years has helped limit the potential contribution Britain could have made. If Brexit succeeds, Britain may not be missed by most of the other countries who have found our lack of interest dispiriting. The EU could, however, benefit from a Britain that finally accepts that its future is in Europe and is willing to engage as a team player with this ambitious project.

6

Requiem For a Nightmare Brexit

THERE IS NO doubt that identity, sentiment, nostalgia and emotion are huge influences in politics. They are extremely complex, very difficult to identify and often impossible to understand or deal with. Analysing or assessing how and why people vote and to what extent the heart or head have helped them come to a decision is fraught with difficulties.

The following extracts from four excellent articles provide invaluable insights into why so many people voted to leave the EU.

1. 'With its attic full of national icons, England can't move on. Scotland can', Ian Jack, *The Guardian*, 25 March 2017.

I climb the retractable ladder and hoist myself through the trapdoor into the loft.

...Here's Winston Churchill as a toby jug, here's a model Spitfire wrapped inside a copy of the *Daily Express*, here's my souvenir coronation mug preserved like a sacred relic since 1953, and here's my great grandfather's medal from the second Afghan war

But now I've got used to the murk, I can see the loft is bigger – much, much bigger – than I thought. That looks like a full-sized Trident missile standing on the mantelpiece, and the real House of Lords where the doll's house used to be. This is such a big loft, in fact, that it can accommodate entire islands – the Falklands, Pitcairn, St Helena and the 11 other British Overseas Territories. There are people too. Some wear red robes with collars of fur. Another, a woman, has a crown. In a debating chamber, men jeer and wave paper at each other.

The cluttered attic is England. You might say Britain, but the essentials are English: the customs, the traditions, the pride in its very old parliament, the cult of the second world war, the anxiety to 'punch above its weight'. 'An unreformable old power' was how the Scottish writer and political theorist Tom Nairn described the UK in 2015, and that seems right. England, the head of the household, never wants to throw out the junk. The House of Commons lives by its old rituals; the House of Lords endures despite a century of tinkering; the winners continue to take all in Westminster's first-past-the-post elections. Submarine-launched nuclear missiles and horse-drawn gold carriages help maintain the country's self-esteem – the second to be used only on special occasions, and the first never at all.

...What Brexit made evident was English nationalism: England v Brussels. One of the great attractions of the first is the prospect Scottish Independence offers for renewal. In terms of the institutions and rituals of the state, its attic is nearly empty. England's rejection of the EU, on the other hand, has come about partly because of the attic, which as the storehouse of tradition will now return to its position as the most sacred room in the house.

...In his new study of populism, *The Road to Somewhere*, David Goodhart attributes the Brexit and Trump revolts to a division in the population between the people he calls the Anywheres and the Somewheres. The Anywheres, typically, are liberally inclined graduates who attended a residential university, found a professional job, and never returned to the place they used to live...They are concentrated mainly in London and other big cities and university towns, and they value 'autonomy and self-realisation before stability, community and tradition'.

By contrast, the Somewheres place a high value on security and familiarity, and have strong group attachments; the older among them pine for a lost Britain. Only a minority have attended university. They are less prosperous than the Anywheres and there are twice as many of them, living mostly in small towns, suburbia and the old industrial settlements, often only a few miles from where they were brought up. Not all of them voted leave – just enough.

Somewheres are attic people, but (as Goodhart concedes) many of us are a bit of both. It's strange now to consider how

English nationalism occupies the role that Scottish nationalism used to have, when Britain represented modernity and Scotland meant Bannockburn: to take us up into the attic and back into the past.

2. *Brexit The Revolt of the Natives: Britain after Brexit 2016,* Anthony Barnett (writer and co founder of open democracy).

Brexit was a wake-up call – but a wake-up call to what? A nightmare of Farage proportions that drags Britain further into an Atlantic of fear and chronic isolation? Or a wake up to mend our broken democracy and heal a profoundly torn society? If you agree we want a society where 'taking control' means our being capable of shaping a future with the rest of the world, not one where we are 'controlled' by our past like a straight-jacket, then we need to understand, I really mean understand, why Brexit happened.

...The forces that lay behind Brexit, each explosive in its own way, shook the world and have started something like a democratic civil war here in Britain.

...Now a new wall has been thrown up across part of Europe. At the moment the barrier is just a declaration. Perhaps it is all the more alarming because its meaning and consequences are still unclear.

...We face the prospect of England being reduced to a self-regarding country, prejudiced and divided, impoverished yet obsessed with money making, separated from Europe's culture and leaving its immediate close neighbours Ireland and Scotland infuriated by our selfish recklessness.

...But neither Britain nor the EU deserves to be pulled apart from each other. The policy problems highlighted by the referendum would all be much better resolved together than separately. On some, such as the environment, peace security, human rights and trade we simply have to share sovereignty with our European partners.

...With respect to the present, for millions who backed leave, their vote was about much more than the EU.

...There were great reasons for the strength and energy of the vote to leave. National identity, political economy, a greedy and indifferent global elite, the collapse of an influential left, the rise of large, wild popular, movements, the lack of real democratic government and the accelerating movement of people internationally all combined to generate the Brexit insurrection.

3. 'The Problem with the English: England doesn't want to be just another member of a team', Prof. Nicholas Boyle, *The New European*, 17 January 2017.

Brexit is the result of an English delusion, a crisis of identity resulting from a failure to come to terms with the loss of empire and the end of its own exceptionalism.

There is a great lie peddled about the referendum: that it expressed the will of the British people.

…The emotion central to the leave campaign was the fear of the alien. The Leave party's unrelenting presentation of the EU as a lethal threat to national identity, indeed as the stranger and enemy, and who had stolen our country, generated emotion. That vision of the EU, worked only in England.

…The end of empire meant an end to all of this. And because England has been unable to acknowledge that loss, it has also been unable to acknowledge the end of English exceptionalism,

The trauma of lost exceptionalism, the psychic legacy of empire, haunts the English to the present day, in the illusion that their country needs to find itself a global role. Of course, it is an illusion: do roughly comparable countries such as Germany or Italy or Japan have such a need?

…England has never wanted to join in the process of growing together, not because it rejects the goal of a super state, which exists only in England's fearful imagination but because it rejects the idea of collaborating with equals – it doesn't want to be just another member of a team, for them it would have to recognise that it has after all an identity of its own.

4. 'Welcome to the Age of Anger', Pankaj Mishra, *The Guardian*, 8 December 2016.

The seismic events of 2016 have revealed a world in chaos – and one that old ides of liberal rationalism can no longer explain.

The election of Donald Trump as president of the United States is the biggest political earthquake of our times, and its reverberations are inescapably global. It has fully revealed an enormous pent-up anger.

The insurgencies of our time, including Brexit and the rise of the European right have many local causes – but it is not an accident that demagoguery appears to be rising around the world.

...There is much dispute about the causes of the global disorder. Many observers have characterised it as a backlash against an out-of-touch establishment. Since the twin shocks of Brexit and the US election, we have argued ineffectually about their causes, while watching aghast as the new representatives of the down trodden and the 'left-behind' – Trump and Nigel Farage, posing in a gold-plated lift-strut across a bewilderingly expanded theatre of the political absurdism.

...And yet we find ourselves in an age of anger. It is a moment for thinkers such as Sigmund Freud who warned in 1915 that the 'primitive savage and evil impulses of mankind have not vanished in any individual', but are simply waiting for the opportunity to show

...We can now see, all too clearly, a widening abyss of race, class and education in Britain and the US.

...Yet a mechanistic and materialist way of conceiving human actions has become entrenched, in part because economics has become the predominant means of understanding the world. A view that took shape in the 19th century – that there is, 'no other nexus between man and man than naked self-interest' – has become orthodoxy once again in an intellectual climate that views the market as the ideal form of human interaction and venerates technological progress and the growth of GDP. The ideals of modern democracy – the equality of social conditions and individual empowerment – have never been more popular. But they have become more and more difficult, if not impossible, to actually realise in the grotesquely unequal societies created by our brand of globalised capitalism.

...Issues of social justice and equality have receded along with the conception of society or community – to be replaced by the freely choosing individual in the market place. But this abstract conception has no room for the emotional situation of real, flesh and blood people – and how they might act within concrete social and historical settings.

...The widespread experience of the maelstrom of modernity has only heightened the lure of resentment.

...For nearly three decades, the religion of technology and GDP and the crude 19th century calculus of self-interest have dominated politics and intellectual life.

With so many of our landmarks in ruins, we can barely see where we are headed, let alone chart a path. But even to get our basic bearings we need, above all, greater precision in matters of the soul. The stunning events of our age of anger, and our perplexity before them. Make it imperative that we anchor thought in the sphere of emotions.

7

The EU, a Case With a Cause:
Going in a Different Direction

IGNORANT ABOUT THE history of Europe, unwilling to distinguish between fact and fiction and lacking any understanding of Britain's search for a role in a rapidly changing world, the Leave campaign became a vehicle for anti-immigration sentiment and a depressing hostility towards foreigners. The core concerns of the radical right in Britain are divisive and a serious distraction from the real problems and challenges facing both Britain and the EU. Ethnic nationalism, xenophobia, authoritarianism and populism are stirring up disaffection and mistrust and creating a divisive, 'us and them' political culture.

The EU has become the focus of concerns about the loss of sovereignty but, again, internationalism, interdependence and a broader humanity require shared aspirations and sovereignty. John Donne's poem, 'No Man Is An Island' spells this out:

> No man is an island,
> Entire of itself,
> Every man is a piece of the continent
> A part of the main.
> If a clod be washed away by the sea
> Europe is the less.
> ...
> Any man's death diminishes me,
> Because I am involved in mankind,
> And therefore never send to know for whom the bell tolls;
> It tolls for thee.

Debunking the myths, lies and distortions around EU membership is vital. This should be accompanied by a positive embrace of the solidarity, stability and security achieved through a peace that has been the hallmark of the countries within the EU since its creation, via the Treaty of Rome, in 1958. Achievements have been significant and the shaping of a new continent has been remarkable.

NATO has played its role in securing the peace of Europe, but this would not have happened without the remarkable achievements of the six original countries who formed the European Coal and Steel Community in 1952, and then the Treaty of Rome, and now a union of 28 countries and 500 million people. There is a great deal to be proud of.

We have short memories. In 1945 Europe lay in ruins, destroyed by war. In 1870, 1914 and 1939, France and Germany were at war. Between 1939 and 1945, militarism, fascism and an ugly nationalism engulfed Europe in a conflagration on an epic scale.

There had to be a way to reconcile the interests of warring nations. Based on the efforts and vision of great post-war statesmen, including Churchill, economic policy, industry, trade and the vision of a Single Market became the building blocks of the now peaceful EU. It is a remarkable success story that is.

45 Years of Success

Celebrating 45 years of EU membership, Britain has made a significant contribution to the widening and deepening of the European project – and could have done much more. As was the case in 1958 when Germany and France provided the leadership in an EEC of six nations, these two countries still provide the drive and inspiration today. Euro-cynics and the right of the Conservative party would have us believe that the existence of the EU has nothing to do with 70 years of peace in Europe.

However, the development of the EU is still a work in progress. Despite recent setbacks in the eurozone and the constraints on further political and economic integration, there is still enormous potential within the EU, which continues to play an important role in the future of Britain and Scotland. Whether Scotland embraces independence, devo unionism or federalism, Europe will be vital for our future.

No Longer Rules the Waves

There are still those in the Conservative party and UKIP who seem incapable of facing up to the fact that Britain no longer rules the waves, controls an empire or has any unique or special relationship with the US.

In the aftermath of the Second World War, the EU has delivered peace, security, prosperity and solidarity in difficult times. Despite the lack of a common foreign policy, evident from the handling of the migration crisis, developments of global significance have taken place.

John McCormick captures in his book *Why Europe Matters: The Case for the European Union* these achievements: the integration of three former dictatorships into the EU and the revival of democracy in Greece, Portugal and Spain; the idea of war between Germany and France now being unthinkable; following the end of the Cold War, the integration of Eastern Europeean countries into the EU; the fall of the Berlin Wall, the collapse of the Soviet Union and the unification of Germany; and on the edges of the EU, nationalism, ethnic cleansing and genocide have been confronted in the Balkans as countries now clamour for membership. Aren't Britain and the British people proud of the part they have played in reconstructing a continent and being part of one of the most important projects in post-war world history? These are remarkable achievements and in Britain we should be proud of the part we played.

Most of Europe has moved from a continent of war to one of peace. This spread of democratic change was recognised with the award of the Nobel Peace Prize to the EU in 2012.

Another important point is that the extreme Euro-cynics fail to explain or even hint at is the degree to which the EU is run by member state governments, Britain included. That Brussels has somehow accumulated independent powers and has the ability to make decisions without the input of national governments or their representatives is an enduring fiction about the EU.

The Euro-sceptics would have us believe the EU is some out-of-control monster desperate to destroy a thousand years of glorious British history. Myth-making on an industrial scale has poisoned the debate on the topic.

Let's look at who runs the EU. Despite the federalist elements of the European Court of Justice and the European Parliament, the 28 member states run the show, in the form of a quadruple lock on how the member states exercise authority and control power. First, every aspect of EU action has to be treaty based, with each treaty having been approved by the heads of Governments in the European Council, each member state's Parliament and, in some cases like Ireland, by referendum. Second, the European Council decides strategic direction and controls the process of integration. Third, the European Parliament is the only Parliament in the western world that cannot initiate legislation – it still has extremely limited powers! Fourth, the Council of the EU, comprising ministers of the 28 member states, works on legislation to be dealt with by the EU Parliament and the Commission; member states control the legislation. Responsibility for the actions of the EU, since its inception, lie with the member states, including Britain.

The ambivalence of successive governments and political parties, especially the Tories, in the period from joining in 1973 has ensured a less than serious commitment to the purpose, progress and potential of this great European project. It now seems paradoxical and somewhat disingenuous to blame all the ills on the EU when Britain and the other 27 countries control the whole operation The perceived problems and weaknesses of the EU are more to do with a detached and uninterested Britain than the Institution itself or the other member states!

EU 'opt-outs' are rarely talked about by the Euro-sceptics. Opt-outs allow member states to withdraw from legislation, treaties and certain policy areas. Britain has more opt-outs that any other country in the EU, covering the adoption of the Euro and Economic and Monetary Union, the Area of Freedom and Justice, the Schengen border arrangements and the lesser known Charter of Fundamental rights which protects citizens and workers in the other member states.

The EU has also led the way in environmental legislation, the protection of employees in the workplace, social rights, human rights and benefits and policies for the family. These measures are viewed by the political right as regulation, bureaucracy and interfering with the market. The EU has protected workers and citizens in periods of Tory Government. Again, the political right don't like this. Tory objections are political, not constitutional or democratic. Britain should be leading in Europe. This is an opportunity for Britain to have a new world view and work with our European neighbours. We need to get over much of our history. Europe is the future.

In the *Financial Times* Philip Stephens wrote that 'the castaway alone on a desert island may be sovereign over all she or he surveys', but is also 'impotent'. He argued, 'A vote to leave the EU would certainly give an instant sugar rush that would feel a lot like an assertion of sovereignty. But a sovereign nation understands that to share what it has in order to get more can be not an act of weakness – but of great strength'.

The Process of Brexit

David Cameron learnt nothing from the Scottish Referendum. Voters were, and still are, being treated like fools, not citizens. Scares and threats have replaced reasoned tempered arguments and, after nearly 45 years of hardly any European debate, British people are being deluged by ludicrous claims and counter claims. On 23 June 2016 the EU referendum was held for the UK to leave or stay and the stakes could not have been higher.

The language of Brexit talked about, 'Putting Britain first', 'making Britain great again', 'taking our country back', 'judges are the enemies of the people' and 'elites establishment and experts are not to be trusted'. The lure of greatness, never defined, was the unspoken mantra of the campaign. A combination of the fanatical and the delusional remain trapped in Britain's glory days of Colonies and empire, where the sun never sets and we, as the US seeks today, ruled the waves and ran the world.

The EU is the most successful institution in the post-war period, but in Britain the Conservatives, from the days of Churchill through Margaret Thatcher to the present day, were always ambivalent about the EU, poor team players and could never adjust to what the other 27 countries felt was progress to peace, stability, security and prosperity. Against this backdrop, the Brexiteers played the immigration card and migrants, asylum seekers and foreigners generally became the target, the scapegoats, an 'outed' group, around which a 'them and us' debate could be manufactured. Again the EU became the source of the problems in what is now a disunited Kingdom. This will all be very familiar to the voters of the US!

The similarities don't end there. Both Trump and Brexit voters, in the main, had the same socio-economic-educational profile and the same grievances. Many people felt left behind, betrayed by globalisation, automation and technology, suspicious of elites and experts, and in the so called 'Rust Belt' areas of both countries, jobs wages and declining labour markets were taking their toll. People had angst, anger and were tired of austerity.

The campaigns had the same language, the same focus on the enemy within created from the enemy without, the votes of angry working people, the sense of hopelessness and political leaders who offered old populism and the old failed policies of yesterday as the antidote to failure in Britain. Within the Brexit campaign the EU was the demon to be exorcised and within Trump's presidency campaign, the 'fake' media, extreme social, economic, religious and racial divisions and a candidate whose disdain and contempt for traditional politics, hit a nerve with over 60 million voters For President Trump this was enough to win but is it enough to govern, if so, for how long?

Politics of Yesterday

The politics of yesterday are being revisited as the echoes of the past grow louder. Britain and the US are bitterly divided nation states. As the levels of political dysfunction grow in both countries, the prospects for a stable Europe are diminished, trade and foreign relations are disrupted and the mixed messages being sent to Putin's Russia are at best dangerous.

There is no disguising the fact that Europe lies astride some of the most volatile and unstable regions of the world. The satellites of the former Soviet Union, Russia, the Middle East, North and sub-Saharan Africa and the countries of Central Asia need consistent and coherent policies. It may be early days but Brexit and the US elections have created fear, mistrust and anger amongst our European allies, NATO and the EU.

Brexit is in danger of moving from a crisis to a catastrophe with all the characteristics of a being on the edge of a black hole with no idea as to what is inside. It should be more accurately described as England voting to leave the EU. Scotland, Northern Ireland and London voted to remain.

Britain is hopelessly divided, and the Government's handling of events is causing further anger and divisions by ignoring the pleas of MPs in the Westminster Parliament for a decisive vote on Brexit after the negotiations are completed, and at the same time ignoring the requests from Scotland and Northern Ireland for their views to be taken seriously. The UK is four nations but only the voice of England is being heard at Westminster, drowning out the voices of the other nations.

Theresa May's trip to the US earlier in 2017, to meet President Trump, only served to underline the dangers that lie ahead. This visit was premature and unsettling in both the policy content and the intent of the two newcomers to office. The reason behind the visit was one of desperation on the part of the British Prime Minister. Seeing, even at this early stage, a potentially empty trading landscape of bilateral negotiations, the loss of EU Single Market and Customs Union membership and the rise of Regrexit – regretting exiting the EU – the Prime Minister, in a panic, sought to reset an old friendship with our enduring transatlantic partner.

There seemed to be a natural synergy between two people who believe in economic nationalism and advocacy of the bilateral 'nation to nation' form of trade which is now so spectacularly outdated. Theresa May had no choice on the matter. For President Trump this is the strategy of White House guru Steve Bannon who described the EU as, 'a flawed institution'.

Putin's Russia is being held up as morally equivalent to western democracies. This may be the world view of the new president, but not one shared in Western Europe.

America First and Britain First are both about nationalism, not patriotism. Every other country has to come second. Britain's transatlantic relations with the US are important on so many fronts, but President Trump's new world of bilateral trade deals, will not usher in a renewed 'Anglosphere' of equal partners, but instead we have the spectaclte of a desperate prime minister struggling for some crumbs off the White House table to create the impression that her brave new Britain, outside the EU, is in the making.

Threat to Britain

Setting aside the wider implications of this approach, there could be real and immediate practical dangers. A hurried trade deal with the US could destroy Britain's farming industry – chlorine washed chicken wouldn't even begin to explain the problems ahead – open up our National Health Service to the predatory behaviour and market excesses of the US pharmaceutical giants and, at least for the time being, Britain would be at the mercy of an erratic and unpredictable president and possibly much worse as time and politics evolve. In Britain there was an explosion of anger over Theresa May's invitation to the new president to visit Britain, unparalleled in modern diplomacy. The Speaker of the House of Commons was unwilling to see the president address both Houses of Parliament and, over one and a half million people signed a petition urging the president to stay away. This outburst of national anger is unprecedented.

Searching for a Role

After divorcing the EU, Britain should be careful about its next partner! Britain has an identity crisis and is still looking for a role. A sense of the scale of challenges facing the world reinforces the added value the EU brings to Britain. Britain's future lies in the EU.

The so-called 'special relationship' with the US-Atlanticism explains much of our current world view in the UK which inevitably spills over into treating continental Europe as lesser players in this Anglo-Saxon hegemony. For the populists and the right in British politics, at least on the surface, this is a struggle to protect our national interest and the absolute sovereignty of the Westminster Parliament. But this is very far from the truth.

Our complex and uncertain view of the EU has significant antecedents which have shaped both Britain's enduring ambivalence towards EU achievements, and that sense of historical purpose the EU has successfully served, since its inception nearly 60 years ago.

Much of the disintegrating UKIP leadership and the extremes of the Conservative party in Westminster hid behind the plausible, but ultimately dishonest, arguments that the EU has stripped away our sovereignty, is undemocratic, bureaucratic, secretive and is not transparent. Despite overwhelming evidence to the contrary, the story then argued that all our ills are the fault of migrants, refugees, Muslims and Eastern European benefit tourists who are simultaneously stealing all our jobs. The story is further adorned by a barely concealed hostility to foreigners, especially the French and Germans who are the supposed ring leaders in the EU's drive towards a federal state. Finally, the story was rounded off with a generous helping of insidious nationalism (mainly English), a dash of isolationism and a hint of racism to come if Brexit succeeds. These cheap patriots are consumed with a misplaced sense of history, and are diminishing Britain in the eyes of the world.

The levels of political dysfunction are growing in both the US and the UK, and the prospects for stable politics are diminishing. Politics is about passion, protest, purpose and principle. A small majority of people may have voted to leave but they didn't vote for the chaos that is now our foreign and trade policy, the new relationship with Trump's America, a conspiracy to dismantle the EU and undermine NATO, to encourage Putin's strategy of weakening these vital institutions or Brexit at any price. The world has changed since June 2016.

The narrative is all important. Fed on a daily diet of distortions, lies and vitriol over the past 45 years it is little wonder that the public have so little information, knowledge and hope upon which to make historic decisions about the future of Britain in the EU or anywhere else. The heart, however, is the home of narratives that arouse the emotions and touch the soul. Compelling narratives are more important in politics than facts, policies, or information. In politics, the side with the best stories – true or false – can gain the upper hand.

Created by a civil war within the Conservative party, promoted by the cheap politics of the UKIP leadership, fuelled by a growing English nationalism, and inspired by a depressing contempt for foreigners, asylum seekers and migrants, this unnecessary EU Referendum debate became dangerous, divisive and dishonest. Never in the history of politics has so much vitriol, hate, lies and distortion been thrown at such a remarkable and successful institution by those on the political right whose politics and party are considered more important than people and principles. Embracing the spirit of Shakespeare's Mark Antony, in the face of the dispiriting state of British politics, our mantra should be: 'We come to bury Brexit, not to praise it. The evil that politicians – men and women – do lives after them.'

There is no case for Brexit. This was increasingly obvious. Boris Johnson's crazed outburst, comparing the ambitions of EU leaders to Adolf Hitler's Third Reich, was further evidence of the desperation of that referendum campaign, all politics and personality with no principles or concerns about people. The history of the EU has been about peace and security. This was all politics with no concern for the people. Johnson's comments were a new low in this debate.

The arrival of Trump and Brexit are providing a wake-up call for progressives in the US and Britain repectively. In both countries, there is growing outrage at what are clearly acts of national self-harm.

Threat to the Union and Scotland's Role In It

Brexit makes no sense, so why should we keep up any illusion to the contrary? Theresa May's fantasies of a world outside the EU are one side of the crisis facing Britain. The other side concerns her crude and clumsy assault on the integrity and importance of the other nations of the Union, in particular Scotland. Brexit has been heavily criticised for offering no alternative future for Britain on leaving the EU.

Throughout Europe electors are in an ugly mood. The rising tide of nationalism, the growth in anti-EU sentiment and the rise of the extreme right in politics should make us wary of where the Brexit campaign is taking Britain. There is an inspiring and positive story to tell about the EU, but it is not being made.

The right in British politics created an elaborate smokescreen of plausible but fraudulent issues to obscure their real agenda which has, for them, more to do with politics, party leadership, protecting the free market, migrants, sentiment and nostalgia.

The EU, in an attempt to create lasting prosperity, has led the way in developing the most successful Single Market in the world, comprising 507 million people: the free movement of goods, services, people and finance; the most progressive and ground breaking environmental and climate change legislation; the most generous aid and development programme; the protection of employees in the workplace; the promotion of social rights and human rights; policies for the family and, despite current set-backs, Economic and Monetary Union and a single currency serving 19 countries.

The EU and the Council of Europe have served the British people effectively through the work of the European Court of Justice and the European Court of Human Rights. These achievements have renewed and shaped a continent and helped Britain prosper and progress in the last half century. There is still a great deal to be done to develop the Social Market – the next phase of the EU – and to develop a common security and migration policy. But these measures, representing over 40 years of progress are resented by the political right and UKIP, and are seen as needless regulation, bureaucracy and interference with the free market. The EU has protected British workers, including periods of Tory Government.

Locked into the Past

Tory and UKIP objections to the EU are political, not constitutional or democratic. They see the complex organisation as a conspiracy against Britain. They see interdependence as interference. They prefer isolationism to internationalism. They remember with affection the days of colonialism, empire and an enduring relationship with the US. They are locked into the past and unwilling to embrace a broader humanity or a new European patriotism.

Lacking any credible or even plausible arguments, Brexit is about the identity, confidence and insecurity crisis that Britain has grappled with for over 70 years. It is about Britain's role in the modern world. It is about the failure of the right of the Conservative party and the UKIP leadership to remove the shackles of the past and set aside the nostalgia, sentiment and delusional mindset that refuses to accept that Britain no longer rules the waves.

We should be having a debate on a new world view built on membership of the EU as a source of prosperity, peace, solidarity and security. These are the benefits of British membership of the EU which isolationists, English nationalists and the deluded right of British politics can't stomach.

The challenges and opportunities of continental Europe have everything to do with us. The spectacle of the Conservative party tearing itself apart over Europe only serves to illustrate how far Britain, and in particular the right wing of the Conservative party, has lost its way in world affairs and political honesty.

On foreign policy, Theresa May seems to have learned nothing from some of our post-war adventures when she said that Brexit Britain and Trump's America can 'lead' the world. Our Prime Minister, heading up a disunited and potentially disintegrating UK, should have more pressing priorities. More to the point, why should Britain want to lead the world?

Britain is a middling country in the world order of international affairs. Despite this the Tories keep looking for a role and seem happy to sup with any devil to maintain the fantasy of still ruling the waves abroad and promoting at home the fiction, so deftly used by Prime Minister Harold MacMillan some 50 years ago, that 'you will see a state of prosperity such as we have never had' outside the EU.

Not content with cosying up to one authoritarian and nationalist 'tough guy', the Prime Minister meets President Erdogan of Turkey, and despite the globally strategic importance of his country, this president jails more journalists than most countries, pays scant regard to human rights and is a seasoned autocrat. The symbolism of this visit is obvious. The substance is harder to discern.

At a time of growing international tensions and challenges the EU is a safe, secure and supportive place for Britain to be.

Most people in Britain would baulk at the idea of the Americanisation of our society, or creating some artificial new Atlantic partnership, or becoming de facto the 51st state of America, or even worse, as Jeremy Corbyn described, a 'bargain basement tax haven off the shores of Europe' where money, markets and the worship of Mammon become the hallmarks of making Britain great again. May and Trump seem content with the notion that countries should be run like companies. This is Trump's key credential for being Commander in Chief, a view reinforced on both sides of the Atlantic by the simple but flawed idea that businesses trade, not countries, and that governments only get in the way. This is an agenda for markets and consumers not for democracies and citizens.

Britain is in danger of helping Trump to break up not only the EU, NAFTA and the Trans-Pacific Partnership but also any other global regional grouping that doesn't meet his requirements of bilateral and unfettered free trade deals between nation states, encompassing all the worst excesses of his autocratic and nationalist impulses. Trump is not a stable or reliable partner.

Churchill and Thatcher: Identity and Ambivalence

The populist leaders of UKIP and the Conservative right, leading the Brexit campaign, have to be classified as cheap patriots; delusional and doing enormous damage to the country by staking out a future that lacks moral purpose, thrives on division and has no vision for the future of Britain at a time of turmoil in World Politics and huge constitutional challenges at home. Europe matters. Britain's future is leading in Europe, not leaving it. This is one of the great success stories of the post-war era, putting aside the nationalism, fascism and militarism of the killing fields of 1870, 1914 and 1939, and pulling in a new direction of security, stability and prosperity and peace. The excesses of the nation state have been contained, and interdependence and internationalism are preferred to isolationism and narrow nationalism.

To obscure the obvious flaw at the heart of the Brexit campaign, Sir Winston Churchill and Margaret Thatcher are often cited to illustrate how revered Tory icons, great statesmen and women and giant patriots, would be supporting the Britain out campaign. The truth, as ever, seems more complex and obscure than the myths being pedalled!

Britain has learned nothing from history and remains as former US Secretary of State Dean Acheson described in a speech at West Point in November 1962:

> Great Britain has lost an empire and has not yet found a role... the attempt to play a separate power role – that is, a role apart from Europe, a role based on a 'special relationship' with the United States, a role based on being head of a 'commonwealth' which has no political structure, or unity, or strength – this role is about played out.

Harold MacMillan was incensed by his remarks and complained to President Kennedy. Acheson was right about Great Britain then and now. This is the identity crisis.

MacMillan persuaded himself that, like other prime ministers before and since there was some mystical bond between the two countries, quite failing to see that 'the United States, like all great powers, would in the end follow – without necessarily much regard for others – what it perceived from time to time to be its own interests' or, as Palmerston said, 'nations have no eternal friends and no eternal foe, only eternal interests'. Britain has an identity crisis and is still looking for a role. A new world view, a grasp of global dynamics and a sense of the scale of challenges facing the world would lead to an appreciation of the added value that the EU brings to Britain and every other member. Our so called special relationship with the US explains much of our current world view and inevitably spills over into treating continental Europe as lesser players in this Anglo Saxon hegemony. The invasion of Iraq may have been an example of misplaced loyalty to a relationship more convenient for one party than special. These are troubling thoughts that lie in the way of developing a much more relevant and beneficial world view of where our interests lie.

Our current complex and often chaotic national view of the EU has significant antecedents which have shaped both our enduring ambivalence towards its achievements and that sense of historical purpose it has successfully served for nearly 60 years. Our enduring commitment to the Transatlantic alliance has overshadowed the nurturing of better relationships with our European allies.

In addition, post-war, Britain has always been ambivalent towards the EU and this is where the speeches of our greatest war time leader Winston Churchill have played a part. Churchill was one of the founding influences of the European project and a passionate advocate of the idea of a United States of Europe. It is worth remembering that Churchill was the first politician to propose a Union of Independent European States. In his famous, 'Tragedy of Europe or United States of Europe,' speech in Zurich in 1946 he said:

> Great Britain, the British Commonwealth of Nations, mighty America – and, I trust, Soviet Russia, for then indeed all would be well – must be the friends and sponsors of the new Europe and must champion its right to live. Therefore I say to you 'Let Europe arise!'

This was reinforced with later remarks.

> [Britain is] a great sovereign state with design and emphasis. For I reject the view that Britain and the Commonwealth should now be relegated to a tame and minor role in the world. Our past is the key to our future, which I firmly trust and believe will be no less fertile and glorious. Let no man underrate our energies, our potentialities and our abiding power for good... We have our own dream and our own task. We are with Europe, but not of it. We are linked but not combined. We are interested and associated but not absorbed.

The path of progress for Churchill was from colonial times, to empire, to Commonwealth, and of course, through friendship with the mighty America. The Soviet Union would never become a 'friend and sponsor of the new Europe'. If this great visionary and statesman was alive today, would he have a different world view and a different sense of where Britain's interests could best be served?

Finally, adding hostility and doubt to questions of identity and ambivalence was Margaret Thatcher. In her Bruges speech in September 1988, she said, 'We have not successfully rolled back the frontiers of the state in Britain, only to see them re-imposed at a European level with a European super-state exercising a new dominance from Brussels'. Protecting the free market and reducing the size of the state were Thatcher's objectives then and they remain the same for much of the Conservative party today. Her objections were political, not necessarily constitutional. To what extent were they constitutional or anti-European?

John Major's Biography

John Major in his autobiography, published in 1999, sheds some light on this. Talking about turns he said, 'Margaret Thatcher, whose later enmity towards all things European became astonishing to behold, unwittingly brought the EU closer by her own actions as PM. In the 1980s she pushed for a truly free market for goods and services across Europe. For in the Single European Act of 1985 she conceded the most dramatic advance of decision making by majority voting – in essence a partial surrender of our sovereignty of decision making in return for a share of pooled sovereignty'. John Major added, 'Returning from her negotiations she commended the agreement in warm terms and it passed through the Commons without difficulty'. How ironic and uncomfortable. Thatcher conceded the greatest giving away of British national sovereignty and the most important EU treaty, Maastricht, was never put to a referendum of the British people, passed only by the House of Commons. Maybe a neoliberal free market anti-big government EU would have changed Thatcher's view on the merits of the EU.

Many Conservative MPs at Westminster, Tory activists in England, and the UKIP leadership despise the EU, the European Court of Human Rights (ECHR), and the European Convention, and have little regard for the Council of Europe. Why is the Conservative party unable to cope with an EU when the other 27 countries can take it in their stride? Why is Britain – or is it England – so uniquely out of touch? Does Germany feel any less of a successful interdependent nation state for taking the EU seriously and sharing sovereignty in areas of common interest and ambition? This myth of absolute sovereignty ignores the reality that, in our interdependent world, Westminster sovereignty has been ceded to Wales, Northern Ireland, Scotland, the EU, the European Court of Justice, the European Court of Human Rights and, in each of the eight referendums, direct power was ceded to the people. This has driven a coach and horses through this archaic thinking.

We should be having a debate on a new world view built on membership of the EU as a source of prosperity, peace, solidarity and security. These are the benefits of British membership of the EU but isolationists, English nationalists and the deluded right of British politics can't stomach any of this. Europe is our future. The challenges and opportunities of continental Europe have everything to do with us. The spectacle of the Conservative party tearing itself apart over Europe only serves to illustrate how far Britain, and in particular the right wing of the Conservative party, has lost its way in world affairs and political honesty.

The Euro-sceptics are dangerous; no case but a very plausible con. Extreme Euro-scepticism, especially from right wing or ultra Conservatives in England and the UKIP leadership, is dangerous, divisive and potentially destructive to the future of Britain. Aided in their intent by right-leaning newspapers and organisations, such as the Churchill Society and Civitas, this conspiracy to remove Britain from the EU should not be underestimated. Anti-EU forces have been at work for 40 years. The EU is complex. Political literacy is underdeveloped in Britain.

The Brexit supporters are vocal and passionate. Their narrative is simple and plausible, but deeply flawed and dishonest. Advocacy of the remarkable achievements and benefits of EU membership has been mooted and at is best ambivalent. The Brexit campaign story is obvious:

- Much of the UKIP leadership and the extremes of the Conservative party in Westminster hide behind the plausible but ultimately dishonest arguments that the EU has stripped away our sovereignty, is undemocratic, bureaucratic, secretive and not transparent.
- All our ills are the fault of migrants, refugees, Muslims and Eastern European benefit tourists who are simultaneously stealing all our jobs.
- There is a barely concealed hostility to foreigners, especially the French and Germans who are the supposed ring leaders in the EU's drive towards a federal state.

- Finally, the story is rounded off with a generous helping of insidious nationalism (mainly English), a dash of isolationism and a hint of racism to come if Brexit succeeds.

Rethinking Our Role in Europe

In the UK we should reflect on what EU politics could be like in the future and not dwell on what it has been like in the past. This has to be the new narrative.

The future of the EU provides such an opportunity for new thinking and a chance for Britain to seriously embrace the European project, strengthen our position at the heart of the EU and accept that our future lies within that great organisation.

Labour should be the pro-European party, more engaged and less ambivalent. Britain's future is in the EU. A more enthusiastic embrace of the EU should also involve a more realistic assessment of our special transatlantic relationship with the United States. This does not mean turning our backs on an alliance that has served us well, but acknowledging that in the new global order, Britain has to be more realistic about weighing up what is in our long-term economic and political interests and how best we can effectively contribute to the global agenda.

Some commentators and historians argue that, since the loss of empire and the emergence of the EU, Britain is still looking for a role in the world. It is highly unlikely that Obama's view of the 'special relationship' differs from his predecessors. From Churchill and Roosevelt, to Thatcher and Regan, to Blair and Bush, the alliance has remained strong.

But does it now matter as much? President Obama confirmed that the US has many 'special relationships'.

At the heart of America's world view, only seen in an extreme form under the Bush administration, lies a number of enduring ideas: a reluctance (first advocated by George Washington) to enter into coalitions; the Monroe doctrine, held since the 1890s, which emphasised the importance of America, the Americas and then the rest of the world, an outlook which sees the US constitution and the institutions of Government as vastly superior to anything the rest of the world has to offer; a sense of nationalism and exceptionalism tinged with a cultural conservatism; a mistrust of the rest of the world; and a naivety and ignorance about how the rest of the world operates outside the American mindset. The election of President Trump has only served to highlight his unpredictability and the prospect that an even deeper sense of exceptionalism will be on offer.

Faced with this powerful set of ideas, which are unlikely to change in the short term, the EU should continue to influence US policy, but start to strengthen, reform and promote a more confident world view, which is less dependent on the US and builds moral authority on a more creative use of 'soft power' and economic strength.

Europe, speaking with one voice on global issues and with the resolve to back words with action, would be a much more credible and effective global player. Recent events, including the Israeli-Palestinian conflict and the Russian-Ukrainian dispute, only serve to reinforce the need for real progress to be made on political integration and foreign policy. The UK Government could play a bigger role in building a credible European voice. Leaving the EU will only diminish Britain's voice and influence. By remaining in the EU, Britain would strengthen the voice of Europe and become a different type of player on the world stage.

Labour has to reclaim the European political agenda in this country. Being at the heart of Europe should be about actions, not rhetoric. Our ambivalence, scepticism and at times hostility towards the EU and its institutions are firmly rooted in the political and popular culture of the UK.

Adding further to the complexity of our relationship with the EU is what might be described as the social protection provided to the British people by the EU when Conservative Government is in power. The Conservatives are incensed with the regulations and directives which offer decent environmental, social, employment and workplace benefits and protection. Part of their thinking about the EU relates to the repatriation of powers to the UK. This is dressed up as winning back the right to legislate for ourselves and not be dictated to by others. This is not the real reason. Much of what emanates from Brussels, both European Parliament and Commission, is progressive legislation which reflects social democracy and the idea of social partnership.

These ideas are alien to modern British Conservatism. Winning back powers 'for the British people' is a cruel deception. This is about politics and philosophy.

Attacking Immigrants

The most disturbing level of Conservative paranoia about Europe is the use of the EU to attack immigrants and whip up a barely disguised form of racism, which is then held up as British jobs for British workers, or defending the health service or benefits system against the Romanians and Bulgarians. These attacks are troubling. They are designed to engender a corrosive dislike of fellow Europeans when all the evidence suggests there is little justification for these attacks and, more importantly, the facts indicate that migrants, in the main, are net contributors to our economy and society. In addition, it was mainly Conservative Prime Ministers such as Margaret Thatcher and John Major who signed up for the Single European Act and the Maastricht Treaty, which created the inspiring vision and strategy of an EU where there would be the free flow of goods, service, finance and people. This was no socialist or Labour plot. Much of the thinking was about the free market and completing the Single Market to let trade flourish in the largest Single Market in the world. All of this is conveniently forgotten by neoliberals who want free markets but object to the consequences of such policies.

On the face of it, and for all the noise surrounding the debate about Brexit, there is a degree of consensus about the best policies to promote Britain's national interests in Europe, if we manage to survive Brexit. The essential difference between the parties is not one of tactics. Labour politicians have generally clothed their desire to repatriate powers, and resist further integration, in the language of commitment and compromise. The Conservatives, by contrast, have attempted to coerce ostensible allies with threats of a British exit from the EU.

The aim of the former Prime Minister David Cameron's European policy was never to protect Britain's best interests within Europe but to appease restive backbenchers. Under his leadership, the Tories withdrew from the European People's Party grouping, abandoning a coalition of the mainstream European centre right for the company of xenophobes, cranks and head bangers.

David Marquand is one of the most respected social democratic academics, a journalist and former MP. In a series of articles for *The Guardian*, he succinctly captures the mood of Conservatives and their enduring dislike of the EU:

Cameron's behaviour is just another chapter in a 60-year-old story. Euro-scepticism, ambivalence, a fondness for empire and an emotional and political attachment to the special relationship with the US have in the post-war period made the channel wider than it is. Not helped by French President Charles De Gaulle saying no to our bid for membership, a lingering mistrust of continental Europe and in particular our old enemy France, an obsession with national sovereignty. The picture is now much more complex as Conservative extremists and the populism of UKIP are bringing a much sharper focus to our membership of the EU as a Union lacking confidence and direction seeks to blame others for our own national shortcomings which in turn is making the UK look mean miserable, intolerant and at time embarrassing.'

'The crisis in Britain's relationship with mainland Europe has its roots in a peculiarly English identity crisis with no counterpart north of the border or west of the Severn. The Scots and Welsh know who they are.

Above all, the English of the 21st century no longer know who they are. They used to think that 'English' and 'British' were synonymous. Now they know that they are not. But they don't know how Englishness and Britishness relate to each other, and they can't get used to the notion of multiple identities'.

'The Conservative party is fighting on so many fronts to ensure it doesn't compromise absolute sovereignty or the fundamental nature of Britishness, whatever that means.'

'This is a time to see the EU as our future and celebrate the contribution of the EU as peacemaker. This is a real success story in terms of both ambition and achievement.'

'This story of Europe might inspire a younger generation who see idealism and inspiration being at the heart of a successful EU'.

'This is an opportunity for Britain to have a new world view and to reorder international and domestic priorities where we work with our European neighbours: this is about sharing sovereignty and ambition. We need to get over much of our history and have a new sense of identity and purpose in this new century. The EU is our future.'

For this to happen, we need to confront the Brexit campaign with a new story for the future of the EU.

The EU is the Role We Are Looking For

Britain has an identity crisis and is still looking for a role. A sense of the scale of challenges facing the world reinforces the added value the EU brings to Britain. Britain's future lies in the EU. The EU Single Market is the largest and most successful in the world, and in volume terms is nearly two trillion dollars bigger than the United States. Maybe the real reason for the current president's EU remarks is envy. The EU, however, should be a cause for celebration on both sides of the Atlantic and not the focus of malice and discontent. Theresa May's vision, of a world outside the EU, is one side of the crisis facing Britain. The other side concerns her assault on the integrity and importance of the other nations of the Union, in particular Scotland. Brexit may yet be the spark that once again ignites the flames of unrest and leads more Scots to think that Britain, under the Theresa May Government and out of the EU, is a poor deal. Faced with this potentially uncompromising reality, Scotland could vote to leave the UK after a membership lasting 310 years.

British people wouldn't welcome the Americanisation of our society or the creation of some rehashed and imbalanced Atlantic partnership or becoming de facto the 51st state of the US or even an off shore, deregulated, low tax and low welfare Britain.

Adapting the slogan attacking Barry Goldwater in the 1964 presidential campaign and applying it to Brexit says it all. Theresa, 'in your guts you know its nuts'.

Nationalism is taking a grip. Populism is its electoral ally. Fake news, attacks on the media and authoritarianism is the method. Truth and freedom are the victims. Isn't it time for Britain and the US, and politicians on both sides of the Atlantic, to make people great again and to put people's interests first?

A new world view is needed. There is an alternative story about the EU but it is not being presented strongly or loudly enough. The EU is not perfect, but solid foundations are now in place for a new progressive century. If anything, after a Brexit we could discover that we are rather less sovereign than we are now. In order to do business, we could find ourselves compelled to bow before rules that, like Norway, we have no say in writing. As the Norwegian conservative, quoted by David Cameron in the Commons, put it:

> If you want to run Europe, you must be in Europe. If you want to be run by Europe, feel free to join Norway in the European Economic Area.

8

Scotland at a Crossroads

FOR A DECADE, the SNP have successfully balanced competent governance alongside their priority and signature issue of Independence. In the eyes of some people, the referendum in 2014 may have been the high water mark of a remarkably successful period, in which they have dominated Scottish politics. For others, post-Brexit, this is only a temporary lull in the battle to 'set Scotland free'. It would certainly be foolish to write off either the SNP or the idea of Independence at this stage. Politics is no longer the comfortable space of the past; shock developments are the norm, volatility is everywhere and Brexit and the right of the Conservative party remain a poisonous and unpredictable threat to the mood of Scotland and the stability of Britain.

The dynamic is now changing. A number of political certainties are being questioned, and for the SNP, domination of the Scottish Parliament is no longer guaranteed.

Questions are being asked about policies in the Holyrood Parliament, including health and education. Innovation and new ideas, have at least for now, dried up. What happens to the new powers the Parliament has gained will be a significant challenge, especially the tax powers.

Further Tory expenditure cuts will impact over the next few years. The party has done well with two significant and charismatic leaders but in recent times they have possibly become overdependent on the cult of personality in the form of a very successful First Minister. This is a critical time for viewing the political landscape of Scotland, the UK and Europe, and reassessing what the options are. The SNP are not by instinct, history, culture or ideology a party of the left, although there is an increasing emphasis to try and take them down this path. They are a populist party, with a significantly inclusive approach. Their excessive discipline, which was a strength for the SNP party over the last decade, could now be a constraint as initiatives are being stifled and there is a look of 'New Labour' in its later stages. Improved prospects for the Tory and Labour parties in Scotland will hopefully deepen and widen both the constitutional and policy debates.

Brexit has completely derailed the momentum of Independence and has certainly put back, by a number of years, the holding of a second referendum. The final impact of Brexit is still to come.

There is now the prospect of a debate on federalism made more real by the improved position of Labour in Scotland after the 2017 general election. The Labour party gained some traction and there is no doubt that there was a significant bounce from Labour's campaign and manifesto. Labour in Scotland are in a much stronger position and are well placed to win back the centre left vote from the SNP, but they have to firm up on an alternative to Independence, firm up on their policy agenda and refrain from sounding like the Scottish Tories. They must promote a centre left agenda on the issues of the Union, on a second referendum in Scotland. There will be a second referendum in Scotland, but not necessarily about Independence. The constitutional question will not go away. Labour must accept the political importance of this and engage more fully in a campaign about federalism. This is the final option short of Independence and its possibilities should be seized by Scottish Labour. Despite the resurgence of the Tories in Scotland there is every possibility that this could be short lived. Scottish Tory MPs are now part of Theresa May's governing party at Westminster and more and more they will be held accountable by Scots for their votes and actions at Westminster, including Brexit. In addition, many of the Scottish Tories by instinct and history are die hard unionists and may be unable to convert readily to a more ambitious federalism, which will require a shake-up of the UK and the radical transformation of Westminster including the provision of a written constitution.

Despite Brexit and the shambolic behaviour of Theresa May's government, it is surprising that the Tories at Westminster have not been buried in an avalanche of questions, exposing both the Government's lack of interest in radical or progressive thinking, as well as reinforcing in the minds of Scots that, whilst constitutional change is temporarily on the back burner, the Tories are still selling Scotland short.

The future of Scotland is politics, politics, politics! Scotland remains divided on its future direction. There is no settled will of the Scottish people, but the EU referendum and the Brexit chaos may be the portent of what a second referendum in Scotland could mean for solidarity, stability and consensus amongst Scots on a way forward.

Much will depend, of course, on Brexit. This is a game changer which could ignite another populist revival in Scotland against this mad idea and, unlike 2014, Scots will be faced with the question of not only leaving the UK but, if Brexit is successful, also leaving the EU. There is no doubt that leaving the Single Market and the customs union and turning our back on the institutions of the EU will also change the dynamic of the economic argument.

The debate on the constitution has been monopolised by the SNP and Independence over the last decade. This is Labour's opportunity, should they wish to seize it. Scots are not yet convinced of Independence as the only way forward, but Independence has built up a great deal of support, momentum, interest and enthusiasm and still runs way ahead of other options. The final destination for Scotland will be influenced more by Westminster and a Conservative government than it will be by Edinburgh. After the recent general election in 2017, the prospect of a Labour victory has become a possibility. Labour will now have a better opportunity to build support in Scotland if they can pursue a progressive, centre left agenda and address the constitutional questions which must open up the federalist option. This is a tough ask. The idea of Independence has been around for a long time and it has made many converts. Is it too late for a federal alternative to gain support and credibility? Are Scots genuinely seeking an alternative to independence and devo unionism?

As we look forward, it is politics that will eventually decide what happens in Scotland, not the economy and not a romantic or sentimental attachment to a Britain that once was. One thing is clear, however, the debate has to extend further than the SNP and the idea of Independence. The next referendum should be about the future of Scotland, not the future of Independence. There is a significant body of public opinion in Scotland that seeks to be convinced of the merits of any of the options. Scotland is currently a 50/50 split on this way forward and this leaves the door wide open. The idea of independence has been around for a long time, and in recent years has gained significant traction, so federalism has an uphill struggle. The idea of interdependence in the EU may have a more attractive ring to it. What now for federalism?

This has to be seen against the wider debate within the UK Labour party. Scotland, with the approval from Westminster, could hold another 'legal' referendum on Independence, but Britain would have to agree to authorise a system of federalism being introduced. The politics of Westminster will be crucial if an alternative to Independence can be found. The stakes are high. Failure could, in the absence of federalism, lead to the break up of the UK. The conversion of Westminster to federalism is complex and cloaked in history. Does Labour have the vision, the energy and the ambition to deliver change?

Labour's prospects look much better after the 2017 general election but there is still a mountain to climb, especially in relation to winning back those traditional Labour voters who feel left behind and who have figured so prominently in the Brexit analysis. If that is possible, the Conservative party's grip on power at Westminster starts to loosen. Labour may then hold the key to unlocking the future of Scotland as well as reinvigorating Britain

This struggle between social democracy and socialism is a problem as old as the party itself, enduring ideas of: managing or taming capitalism or replacing it; social democracy or socialism; party or parliament and people; party membership or parliamentary party; protest or power; reform or revolution; and democracy or direct action, have all dominated Labour debates since its creation, but there is more to this than ideology or policy. Labour has drifted from having a sense of a historic mission or deeper purpose. There is no vision for 'our' better tomorrow, a widening gap between the generations, growing inequality and a profound sense of 'them and us'. The excesses of globalisation, austerity economics, neoliberalism, and the relentless inroads of market principles into our social and public realms merely confirm capitalism has not been effectively managed. People are suffering and they are angry. People's feelings of betrayal, broken promises and lack of trust are screaming at us from every possible direction. Right wing populism is filling the political space.

There is now a struggle for the heart and soul of the Labour party and there is no easy or obvious way to reconcile differences. The Parliamentary Labour Party has much to learn. Too often the PLP appears remote from the public and seems soulless, technocratic and managerial. They are law makers and need focus but not in a way that leaves party members and the public on the margins.

Corbyn has shaken us from our complacency, boosted membership and enthused young people, but a great swathe of electors and much of the PLP remain disconnected and unconvinced.

This political alliance of party members, Parliamentary Party and the people isn't working! Jeremy Corbyn has halted Labour's decline, but the question is: Can he deliver on its long term recovery? There is no place in or around the Labour party for the political baggage – the tactics, style, tone or intolerance – of the hard left. It is worth pointing out that MPs are political representatives, not party delegates, and Labour is a party, not a cult. Momentum is looking more and more like a party within a party.

Bernie Sanders, uncharacteristically for the US, ran on a socialist ticket, fired up the base of a conservative Democratic party and enthused and inspired young people to become involved. There are parallels with Corbyn. Promoting anti-austerity economics, tackling inequality, protecting employment rights, building a national education service, bringing the railways back into public ownership and keeping the NHS free from privatisation have as much to do with common sense as they have to do with socialism. These are popular with the voters. These are unifying policies.

Tony Wright, former MP and distinguished academic, identifies the essence of Labour's current dilemma:

> Corbyn's successful leadership campaign was based on telling people what the Labour party stood for and what it would do. Members and supporters viewed this as being both refreshing and overdue. People were thinking aloud, the word socialism was heard at rallies and there was talk of humanity, ethics, equality and fairness. This had echoes of the Scottish referendum campaign where people felt empowered, enthused and were not content to be subdued by old electoral habits or what was on offer from the traditional political parties or to be intimidated by the establishment. Ideas and ideals matter. They represent the building blocks from which a new political narrative can capture the hearts and minds of an electorate that have little understanding of who Labour is, what the party stands for, what does it aim to do and how will these be achieved.

Labour cannot continue in its present form without a successful political alliance – the party membership, parliamentary party and the people – finding a way to coexist and win power. This is vital to the future of a party that is interested in both protest and power.

Labour needs:

- A public philosophy to compete and contest the market philosophy of the Tories and built around a series of unifying themes.
- And a political creed, which we do not have and which leaves people confused and mistrustful of what we stand for. Our lack of clarity as a party is debilitating. RH Tawney, writing in 1932, outlined his reasons for the dramatic defeat of the party in 1931 and how this could be turned around in the future. For Tawney the problem was, 'a lack of a creed', not a rigid doctrine but: 'a common conception of the ends of political action, a means of achieving them, based on a common view of the life proper to human beings and of the steps required at any moment more nearly to attain it'.
- A creed in the form of formal statement of shared beliefs – a set of aims which guide the actions of a party. The modern Labour party doesn't have a creed, operates in a complex social, economic and political world without a well defined moral compass. This may be changing. The leadership of Atlee and Thatcher had a creed, a political purpose and a transformative agenda.
- An embrace of both policies and action required to achieve them instead of endlessly debating abstract notions. A commitment to change.
- A much clearer offering of what the party stands for which will aid credibility, clarity and relevance. And indeed radicalism.

For Labour, the press mood is harsh and unforgiving. The party will have to dig deep to find a new way forward and accept that party membership, while important, is only one element of the political alliance needed to translate passion and protest into power with a clear purpose. Labour needs to redefine the British political conversation, or the nationalists and populists in England and Scotland will continue to define it for us.

9

Scotland – the Story So Far

THERE HAS NEVER been a time in UK or Scottish politics where there is such a need for some decisive constitutional leadership, new thinking, and action. A pointless and cynically opportunistic general election held on 8 June has provided a spectacular outcome. Labour offered an attractive, progressive, and relevant manifesto, an inspired message of hope, and secured, against all the odds, a remarkable share of the vote, which now opens the prospect of a general election victory, possibly even within the next year. The battle for Britain is now in play.

While the nightmare of another Tory Government is now a reality, this may be short lived. The Conservative party is running on empty. Only a political party operating on the margins of credibility would join up with the DUP. After the worst election campaign in modern times, Theresa May is the equivalent of the walking dead. She has no credible mandate and during the campaign exhibited the signature features of modern conservatism: arrogance, complacency, hubris, exceptionalism and exuded that lure of greatness and entitlement of a party born to rule. More than that, her shambolic handling of the Tory manifesto and its divisive content spoke volumes about what kind of post Brexit future she envisaged for Britain.

This was a good result for Labour in what is now a massively complex and uncertain future for the UK. In addition to Brexit, where the social, international solidarity, terrorist and defence dimensions need to be given more prominence alongside the economy and trade, many other important issues demand scrutiny, debate, and an injection of new thinking.

The Scottish results in the 2017 general election hold out the prospect of a different kind of debate in the future. The fortunes of the major political parties are changing. The Tories and Labour made gains in terms of seats and the share of the popular vote and the SNP has now to acknowledge that for a variety of reasons, political life will be less straightforward and much more complex. In this regard Scotland – its politics, democracy, and governance – must become less insular, partisan, and open to a wider and more inclusive constitutional debate in which the future of Scotland is no longer debated solely in terms of the SNP, independence and devo unionism.

There is a new debate to be had which can break free from the binary choices of 2014 and 2016 – divisive, partisan, and inconclusive – which have in turn created binary mindsets. Scottish politics can be very insular. There is a need to acknowledge the wider politics of Europe in what we do. The SNP have dominated Scottish politics for a decade and Independence is firmly rooted in the public discourse, but there is still no conclusive outcome to where Scotland goes next on its constitutional journey. Scotland remains divided, and party votes may be different from yes/no votes of the Independence Referendum.

On 8 June 2017, many Scots embraced Unionism in their votes for Labour and the Tories. The analysis and the assumptions, however, may not be as simple as that. John Curtice, incisive as ever, said in a post-election *Herald* article that, 'support for independence may not translate to votes for the SNP'. As the volatility of Scottish politics has intensified, so has the complexity of the constitutional question, especially in the context of Brexit. Support for independence may come from voters of other parties and this is why it is difficult to read across from the 2014 Independence Referendum to voting intentions in general elections.

The idea that voting for the SNP is the only way of supporting an independent Scotland may be flawed, as is the notion that some of those who vote SNP could not be attracted to a federalist future. Labour's obsession with a narrow form of unionism may have undermined their pursuit of socialism and distorted their appeal. The constitutional question is much more fluid than we think, but in this polarised, and at times ill-tempered political environment, negativity, intolerance and narrow mindedness prevails. This is the time for a different debate.

Despite the Tories winning second place in Scotland, there is an obvious ceiling to their aspirations. They represent deep-seated unionism; geographical and historical concentrations of electoral support and have benefited from, and have been able to hide behind, the more progressive politics of the Scottish Parliament. Ruth's 13 will now be part of Theresa's Parliamentary group at Westminster and become accountable for what they do under a more aggressive media spotlight. What kind of Conservatism will they be a voice for?

For the longer term, the more significant and unexpected result was Labour's increased share of the vote and the gain of six seats. Boosted by the success of Labour's manifesto and the UK campaign, the party in Scotland must recognise that progressive policies through the prism of socialism or social democracy may have attracted more support than any opposition to 'Indy Ref 2'. For far too long Labour in Scotland has been a critic, but rarely a positive contributor to the constitutional debate. This should end. There are different views within the party, as evidenced by opinion polls. Federalism is a viable option, but it needs to be promoted and debated. Talking about the future of Scotland is not just talking about Independence. At a basic level, the Scotland question will not go away. Saying no to democracy will not help either. The conditions are now opportune for Labour to take the lead. The SNP's gloss is fading; 10 years is a long time in Government and policy issues are catching up on them and adding to their vulnerability.

Scottish Labour's challenge is to persuade, or possibly demand, that if a Labour government wins power in the next few months or years, there must be a commitment to a written constitution for Britain. Removing power from Westminster to the people, a federal UK and, at an appropriate time, a referendum on this constitutional alternative and another referendum on the outcome of the EU negotiations.

Crucially for Britain no one appreciated how quickly our new Prime Minister, Theresa May, would become an enthusiastic convert to the fanatical and delusional behaviour of the extremes in her party. Her reckless and arrogant approach to the Article 50 process may be playing to her base, whatever that is, but it has also shown her contempt for the nearly 50 per cent of the population who voted to remain and the distinctive votes of Scotland and Northern Ireland.

Almost half of the UK voted to remain but the Prime Minister acts like they don't exist: 16 million extras in a fake drama! By ruling out the 'free movement of people' and, by default, taking us out of the Single Market and the Customs Union, a hard Brexit will lead Britain closer to a political black hole. Few people believed that the destructive attitude in her party towards the EU would continue under her leadership. How wrong we were.

Her ill-advised trip to see President Trump revealed both the vulnerability of the PM's increasing isolation, her willingness to be identified with economic nationalism, and her desire to embolden right wing populism in the US and Europe. Has supping with the new political devil in World Politics also revealed her ideological solidarity with Trump's views of the EU and immigrants. Trump to Erdogan are populist political 'hard men' who see the EU as an external threat to their ambitions for authoritarianism; we should maybe judge people by the company they keep. Populist extremists of the right and left seem to be comfortable with each other. In the US there are congressional inquiries into Russian involvement in the Trump campaign but no action in Britain about interference in our European Referendum. Why not?

Theresa May is also undermining the fragile constitutional make-up of the UK by her abrasive and uncompromising attitude towards Scotland and Northern Ireland. Despite her warm words and gestures, the PM shows no real interest in or understanding of life beyond Westminster. She is, in a determined and single handed way, stirring political unrest in Scotland, sowing the seeds of discontent and creating the conditions for a second referendum. Her extraordinary outburst about First Minister Nicola Sturgeon 'playing politics' seems hypocritical, as does the perverse comments about why the same arguments she deploys for leaving the EU cannot be used by Nicola Sturgeon to explain her reasons for leaving the UK. There is a new political dynamic in place. Unlike 2014, where being in the UK provided membership of the EU, the parameters of the debate have dramatically changed. A different set of choices and priorities have been created by Brexit.

For Scotland's First Minister, Theresa May is the political gift that just keeps giving. A new Prime Minister held out the prospect of change but she became consumed with the madness of Brexit. For the SNP, the prospect of an early Independence Referendum has faded. This has led to much anxiety, disappointment and heart searching amongst party members, especially young supporters, about what would happen next. The First Minister had no case to go early as there was no prospect of victory.

Theresa May then came to the rescue. The polls have shifted and so has the mood in Scotland. Theresa May now faces a crisis of her own making. This confirms a widely held view that the momentum for radical constitutional change will not come from the passions and protests of Holyrood alone, but from the complacency, indifference and political blunders of Westminster. What result would represent the 'settled will' of the Scottish people? What do Scots really want? Our democracy is imperfect.

Northern Ireland has been treated in a similar fashion. The outcome of the recent election has the potential to create another nightmare for Theresa May. Showing scant regard for Irish history, and the anger of another Remain group being ignored, the PM is faced with a new debate about the six counties becoming part of a United Ireland. Political momentum for this has been boosted by Sinn Féin and the Social Democratic and Labour Party (SDLP) being, for the first time, the largest political grouping at Stormont. Once again it adds to the view that our Prime Minister is closeted away in another dimension and has taken leave of her senses. By her own political convictions, her political inexperience, or the pressures being exerted by the zealots of the ultra-right in her party, or a combination of all three, she is dismantling and diminishing Britain from within. This is a disunited kingdom heading towards economic and political chaos, and a Prime Minister being allowed to get away with it.

We seemed to have reached a point where Theresa May is still willing to pay any price to leave the EU, despite her protest on the contrary. Britain has to recognise the possibility of a damaged Britain and so does the Labour party whose behaviour is confusing their own supporters and whose actions at times seem indistinguishable from the Tories in their approach to Brexit. Labour has to change course and lead the assault on Brexit.

In the US, people are hearing President Trump lie to them everyday and witness him taking executive actions that hurt and betray the people who voted for him, instead rewarding the rich and powerful. In Britain people are being lied to as well. The very people who felt left behind in the North and who voted to leave will suffer most. Like Trump, the Tories always help their own.

For working people, in Scotland and Britain, there are no rewards from Brexit. Like Trump, Theresa May will hurt the very people she promised to stand up for. Fake news, propaganda and lies in this so called post-truth era, are destroying the basis of public discourse in Britain. No EU. No Single Market. No Customs Union. No effective opposition in what is a modern version of the Battle for Britain. Theresa May is currently the Prime Minister of all of the UK. She needs to forget the lure and language of greatness and remember that England is dragging Britain out of the EU, and is now the only voice being heard at Westminster as the concerns of other nations are drowned out.

The country is undergoing a dramatic political transformation, but this shouldn't be the sole preserve of the SNP. The rest of Scotland has to join the debate in order to give balance, clarity and constructive criticism to an idea that is dividing Scotland and where big questions need further debate.

The Brexit campaign has shown that a referendum producing a small and insignificant majority relative to the scale of the issue and the size of the population, could have disastrous consequences. Scotland must learn lessons. To be independent in the full constitutional, sovereign and political sense requires a much greater degree of consensus and a greater understanding of what the consequences might be. A greater proportion of Scots need to be convinced that they are clear about what is best for Scotland. Brexit is dangerous and divisive. Slim majorities can undermine national solidarity, cohesion and stability and the bitter legacy that befalls the defeated and the discontented can be enduringly destructive. The idea of independence or interdependence in Europe has a positive ring to it, but in the light of a nation 50/50 divided on a way forward and where there is no settled will of the Scottish people, other ideas and options may emerge. This is the big challenge for Scotland.

Setting aside the financial issues of currency, the current fiscal imbalance, and the other economic issues that so heavily influenced the outcome of the 2014 Referendum, raw politics will play a bigger role in any future debate. The concept of nation building, involving institutional development and capacity building, require more serious attention. For the vast majority of Scots who are not 'be a nation again' or 'independence at any price' supporters of Independence, more work has to be done on what Scotland could be, and spell out what that might look like. This is regardless of Independence or federalism. Our constitutional debate requires a bigger, wider and more inclusive audience. The SNP, may include many supporters who might support federalism. There is no reason why the SNP shouldn't reach out to the other parties and offer the prospect of building a progressive alliance to deal with our collective future. Scotland is a divided nation; in recent years, opinion polls, real elections and the referendum of 2014 have shown this. This strengthens the case for a wider, deeper and longer debate which may help to build a consensus. Weighing up the crucial importance of another vote, there is no reason why this has to take place in this session of the Holyrood Parliament. Caution is required. Until the case for Independence, or indeed for any other constitutional idea, is more widely rooted in the hearts and minds of Scots, a new vote may not settle anything. Some will argue that a win only requires a one vote margin, and this is what democracy means. Constitutional questions demand more serious consideration. This is where we need a new politics.

In recent history, whenever there has been an upsurge of nationalism, Unionism has responded but never with an overarching vision of the future of the UK and Scotland's role in it. Scotland stirs and Westminster responds, but only with more powers. But how many more times can powers be offered to Scotland when nothing changes at Westminster and we keep slowly but perceptibly drifting towards Independence? The UK government, and the traditional parties, have never grasped the seriousness of the constitutional issue and the transformative change that is taking place in Scotland. The political energy released during the Referendum campaign in 2014, a much less trusting and volatile electorate, crumbling political loyalties and a new confidence, have created a new politics in Scotland and we are not certain where any of this is leading. To slow down or halt the surge of the SNP is one idea, but the bigger issue is getting the constitutional question resolved with as much consensus as possible.

But where is the vision at Westminster? This is a serious question. Why can't Westminster abandon its unwritten constitution that allows 650 MPs and 1000 Lords to dominate at the expense of the people and four nations of the Union? The Unionist parties still fail to understand what Scots were saying on September 18 2014. The antidote to a failing union is a political transformation. It is about a declining Union, a new narrative for Scotland's future and a new role for Scotland in a transformed UK. This is really not so complicated, but it requires Westminster to acknowledge that the public debate in Scotland is well beyond just more powers from Westminster; it is about shared sovereignty, identity, social democracy and a better future. More fundamentally this is about trust and politics, not more taxation and powers.

People are looking for vision and a sustainable, long term and viable alternative to Independence and that is where home rule or federalism enters the debate. But let us be in no doubt that if we are unable to coalesce around a real alternative to Independence, then we are merely moving slowly but surely towards the removal of Scotland from the UK. This becomes a matter of when, not if.

From the late 19th century to the early part of the last century, for Gladstone and the Liberals and the socialist icons like James Maxton, Home Rule was viewed as the sensible way to keep Scotland in the Union and on very different terms to the Union of 1707. The Ireland question allowed some remarkable debates to take place at Westminster around the late 1880s and the early 20th century. These debates were crammed full of vision and, in many ways, talked about issues that are even more relevant today than they were a 100 years ago. It is now time to make those dreams a reality. Federalism is now the key to a bigger debate.

Where does this leave Scotland? Scotland could see a form of federalism, independence or some other, as yet unknown, four nation constitutional solution. Regardless of the outcome, an Independent Labour Party (ILP) in Scotland is essential. This could be part of modernising the UK party. We need a federal structure in which the new ILP could be a sister party, similar to what has happened in other parts of Europe. The Scottish Labour party is still dominated by the interests of London, Westminster and English politics. Despite the changes brought in by Jeremy Corbyn, reform of UK Labour is long overdue. The ILP imprint would send a powerful message of Scottish identity and politically distinctive policies.

There is an urgency to this. The SNP are at their lowest point in a decade. The Tories are unconditional unionists, and Labour is within reach of victory at Westminster, but circumstances could change. The SNP, as the now established voice of Scotland, will remain the lightning rod for grudge and grievance politics and the anger, uncertainty and volatility which is driving the politics of western democracies. If Labour believes that there is a real and viable alternative between Tory devo unionism and the SNP's independence, why wait? Labour has stubbornly remained with the idea that there is more to political life than the constitutional question. They are right on this, but since the issue of identity has become such an influential part of the public discourse in Scotland, Labour will not break through until it has a viable alternative to Independence which will capture real and lasting support.

Scotland's immediate future, with political populism coalescing around national identity, looks less clear. While Nicola Sturgeon continues to run political rings around Theresa May in terms of competence, the question of timing becomes a major headache for Scotland's First Minister. That said, the comments from the First Minister offering to delay a second referendum if there was a soft Brexit strengthens her position. There seems little likelihood that the Prime Minister can deliver a soft Brexit, caught as she is between the rock of the fanatics and the delusional on the right of her party, and the hard place of immigration and the clamour to reject the 'free movement of people'.

The immediate consequences for Scotland moving into a new and potentially turbulent period are hard to pin down, but one thing is clear: deciding Scotland's constitutional future will not be easy. Brexit has changed the parameters and dynamic of the debate on Scotland's future, and maybe for the best.

For nearly a decade, Scottish Labour has been forced on to the defensive over the future of Scotland. Brexit has shown that Scotland has no real political power in what remains a Britain dominated by the ideas of absolute sovereignty, exceptionalism and the inertia of a Westminster mired in the politics of the past and an increasingly authoritarian mindset. Power devolved is not power shared. If change is to mean anything then the crucial question becomes: What would a federal union look like?

Theresa May has abandoned the illusion that Scotland or Northern Ireland or Wales matters. England is now the problem – this was after all an English Exit – and the Conservative party has demonstrated that it is not a team player. The Tories cannot cope with the EU and feels the other nations of the UK are more of a political inconvenience than an asset. The devolution of more 'powers' is not a solution when real 'political power' is not on offer.

Unless Labour can reoccupy the constitutional space, create a new and relevant narrative for Scotland's relationship with the UK, and embrace the desire of Scots to see a way through this constitutional impasse, the party will continue to struggle. It is the elephant in the room. The party has so much positive history and a great deal to contribute to the politics of today and tomorrow. Labour has to get to grips with the Scotland question. This is the key to unlocking a way back for Labour and sending a powerful political message to Scots that the party now understands, for the first time in at least a decade, that the politics of nationality, identity and self-determination matter.

The 2016 Holyrood election was unionism and nationalism at work with Labour in a political and constitutional no man's land and squeezed by stark but successful political tactics. Despite SNP claims to the contrary, this election was not about 'bread and butter' policies of tax, health and education, or the notion that Independence was on the back burner, or we had to move on from the constitution. This was a clever and successful trick. The post Scottish referendum mood and the 45% campaign for yes was evident as the constituency vote for the SNP delivered far more seats on a similar share of the vote than in 2011. This time, unlike 2011, the SNP couldn't maintain the Regional or List vote and lost the chance of an overall majority. For the Scottish Tories this was a highly successful forage into constitutional politics. The Tory Leader exhorted voters to move beyond constitutional issues and the idea of another referendum. This was again a successful deception. Tories voted for the Union. Tories who had flocked to the SNP in 2007 and 2011 returned to the fold, their mission to damage Labour was no longer required. Ruth Davidson skilfully exploited the Regional or List system and boosted the number of Tory MSPs to propel her party in to the official opposition slot. Many Labour voters stayed at home but a number would have been drawn into voting for the SNP or the Tories.

Labour learned lessons, Scotland's politics were becoming more fluid and, in a different context, the 2017 general election revealed a slight recovery in its electoral fortunes.

Both the SNP and the Tories are claiming to be the authentic voice of Scotland. This was about the new mood of Scotland where two of the opposing forces in the Independence referendum were once again battling it out on constitutional and political lines. Labour doesn't have a constitutional position other than the ill-advised vows and more powers. Saying no to Independence is not a solution or a strategy and the electors see through this. The current Westminster settlement for Scotland could lead to Independence.

Labour also needs to understand that the Scotland question is more than vows, powers, unionism or nationalism. This is a battle for the hearts and minds, soul and spirit, sentiment and traditions of an ancient nation and a modern country. These are not the abstract or philosophical footnotes to the history of a nation, but the building blocks of Scotland's DNA.

There is a rationale and logic to the compelling view that Scots don't want the constitutional question to carry on for decades. Post-

Independence Referendum the mood is still with the SNP and a shaky embrace of leaving the UK. The recent general election has revealed a slight resurgence of Tory Unionism, but every opinion poll shows that Scotland is now bitterly divided and we are a 50/50 nation; in this titanic struggle for a new and enduring constitutional settlement, Labour must now lead. Is there an attractive, sustainable, workable, coherent and popular alternative to independence and grudging Union concessions? Is a form of home rule, four nation federalism, interdependence not independence, a possible way of keeping Scotland in a new Union?

UK Labour could help Scottish Labour. The politics of Scotland and England are rapidly diverging. English nationalism is at war with Scottish nationalism. Labour in Scotland is trying to find traction between nationalism and unionism. Post 2014 Scottish referendum Scotland is a different political place. Glasgow has become a special political problem helped by Labour's inability to debunk the myth that the SNP is a progressive centre left party. Scotland needs an independent voice, not necessarily a voice for Independence.

In 2007, 10 years on from the historic Scotland White Paper published in 1997, Tom Brown and myself co-authored, *Scotland the Road Divides*. We said, 'the maintenance of Scotland within the Union can only be achieved if politicians across the Unionist spectrum are prepared to be open minded, face up to uncomfortable truths, shed outdated prejudices, realise the need for new political ideas and accept pragmatic solutions'.

We added, 'the party that delivered devolution has not come to terms with its consequences' and that 'Labour should be redefining its mission in post devolution Scotland, rethinking the party's identity and whether it should be more Scottish'.

We asked, 'Does it want to create a distinctive political culture and identity – or does it want to continue to look over its shoulder to Westminster?'

Sadly, the question remains unanswered and the ideas hinted at have largely been ignored.

Our Changing World

First Minister Alex Salmond set out the challenge, in his inaugural speech at Holyrood on 23 May, 2007, when he said, 'Scotland's new politics starts now'. This of course predated the financial and economic crisis of 2008, the rise of right and populism in western democracies. The decline of support for traditional parties – in 1955, 98 per cent of the population voted Labour or Conservative, the figure for 2015 was 39 per cent – and the emergence of nationality and identity politics have added to the unpredictability of voters. A series of political earthquakes in Scotland have transformed the landscape and the SNP – both populist and nationalist – continues to dominate all levels of politics.

Throughout Britain, Europe, and the US, the anger, the anxieties, fears and resentment of voters grew as inequality deepened and millions of people struggled to cope with austerity and felt excluded. A bewildering pace of change has engulfed our politics and created a volatile and fragile electorate, where traditional allegiances and loyalties, and other certainties, have been shredded.

The world of politics has changed, for ever. Life has evolved. Society is more complex and immersed in a digital revolution. Socialism and social democracy are under attack throughout the EU. The very idea of democracy is being questioned. Scotland has become a very different nation, wrapped up in a new agenda. Remarkably, though, and often defiantly, Labour in Scotland seems unable to understand the constitutional crisis engulfing the party.

Labour's decline has been evident over the last decade but there are signs that this is changing. There has been a failure to adapt to the new realities of a more confident and questioning Scotland, and a declining and disunited kingdom. The constitutional question, which has always been difficult for the party. Labour sees the problems and challenges of 21st century Scotland through the prism of 20th century Westminster politics: Scotland has found its identity but the Labour party is struggling to find theirs.

More in sorrow and bewilderment, than in anger and resentment, people would like to vote Labour, but they still question who or what the party stands for. Deep and enduring historical ties have been shattered, decades of loyalty have disappeared and people are genuinely perplexed as to how the party has fallen so far behind. How does a political party reinvent itself?

Facing the Future

The Labour party must escape the suffocating agenda of Westminster and start to talk up a narrative for the new Scotland which addresses the issues people are concerned about, including the constitution; it must be presented in a different tone, style and language and appear less angry in its outlook and delivery. So where does the party start?

Being credible, by being honest on the constitutional question and recognising the party is split, but also acknowledging the simple fact that it will be Labour voters who will ultimately decide Scotland's future in what is a bitterly divided country, split 50/50 on the big issue.

Campaigning honestly about Brexit and spelling out its catastrophic consequences for Scotland, being unapologetic about Scotland's Remain credentials and unconvinced that Brexit is inevitable.

Explaining what federalism and four nation politics looks like. This could be a reality or are we merely whistling in the dark?

Showing our broader humanity, our internationalism, and our embrace of 'difference' and diversity.

Arguing for an Independent Labour Party (ILP) in Scotland, if the party is ever to become the voice of Scotland, in or out of the Union.

Making sense of nationality and identity politics. People are entitled to have multiple identities;

Questioning our unconditional love affair with the old Union. England does need a voice, but not by dominating Westminster. The politics of England and Scotland are diverging: Brexit is an England phenomenon. A slavish embrace of the old Union doesn't make sense.

Spelling out the challenges of automation, technology, the digital revolution and robotics, and their impact on jobs and skills in Scotland.

Campaigning against the excesses of market forces and instead promoting the common good.

Debunking the idea and the impression that being a proud Scot is incompatible with being a good socialist or social democrat.

Acknowledging the fact that the worst is yet to come if a Theresa May landslide fans the flames of further constitutional unrest in Scotland, and her authoritarianism and economic isolation find little favour.

Understanding the need to make ambition and aspiration matter, by building a mood, momentum and a movement that once again captures the imagination of Scots.

Countering the widely held perception that we don't appear to be Scottish enough and rarely act as the voice of Scotland.

Remembering the Tories are also our political opponents especially the right wing group of fanatical and delusional Tory and UKIP Brexiteers who see the break-up of the Union and the catastrophic economic consequences for Scotland and Britain as a price well worth paying for their madness.

Supporting democracy by dropping our opposition to a second referendum. It is going to happen sometime and trying to avoid it will not defeat Independence or make it go away. Instead we should hold out the prospect of an alternative way forward;

Making inequality, which is poisoning our society, the issue of our time. Yes, the big economic levers are at Westminster but we are making little impact in health, education, and public services in Scotland. Representing working people in Parliament and pursuing a fair and just society were Labour's founding priorities in 1900.

On reflection, this is not the stuff of Einstein, but a candid and quite basic attempt to help recast Labour's mindset and help reinvent a party with style and substance and the great principles upon which the party was built: these remain as relevant and credible today as they were in 1900.

Two vital questions will dominate Labour's future. What does the party stand for, especially at a time when the SNP are attempting to steal their clothes? What is Scotland's future relationship with the Union?

Creed and Constitution

After the disaster of 1931, when the Labour government, overwhelmed by financial crisis, had suffered a political disintegration from which it took many years to recover, RH Tawney talked about the future of the party in his famous article, 'The Choice before the Labour Party'.

He believed the party's fundamental problem was its 'lack of a creed'. He argued this was the basis of all its other difficulties. A creed is not a rigid doctrine but 'a common conception of the ends of political action, and of a means of achieving them, based on a common view of the life proper to human beings, and of the steps required at any moment more nearly to attain it'. This, he added, required a firm intellectual and moral foundation, without which the party would lose its way.

Setting aside the dated language, but not the content, the lack of a 'creed' is fundamental to Scottish Labour's difficulties. Talking about 'our values' in a vague and general way just underlines the emptiness and the lack of ideas generally in Scottish politics. Labour can only flourish when it offers something that people can believe in.

The Scotland question is more complex and remains a debate that divides the Labour party. There is no reason why they shouldn't be acknowledged and accepted. Without credible arguments or ideas the party will remain torn between independence and a devo unionism.

A federal constitution for Britain, the only real alternative, goes largely unnoticed, has failed to gain any traction, and is viewed by many as too little and too late. The prospects of federalism and a new written constitution emerging from Westminster any time soon, and supported by either Labour or the Tories, are hard to imagine.

Labour's understandable desire to get back to debating the big issues, such as education and health, will be frustrated if they cannot find a way through the less comfortable undergrowth of the constitution, which has marginalised any serious policy debate in Scotland for some years now and which is likely to dominate the general election. It won't go away.

Time for Action

Breaking free from the past, but retaining timeless principles and the history that fired the party and shaped its creed, is the way forward. The nearly three quarters of a million people who voted Labour in the SNP landslide in 2015 deserve reassurance, a bigger stake in deciding Scotland's future and a more tolerant, confident, optimistic, and positive party.

Ideas matter. They provide the basis of a political narrative and a public philosophy. Ideas explain how the world is and how it might be changed. They define ends and identify means. Ideas are the basis for rebuilding trust, capturing the imagination of people, especially the young, and winning the hearts and minds of electors.

So, what would this look like? What are the constitutional issues the Labour party should adopt:

- Supports 'real' federalism and four nation politics.
- Campaign against Brexit. Derailing and defeating the legislation must be the main aim. The Scottish Parliament, the Scottish Government and the progressive political parties should work together to achieve this outcome.
- Argues that the constitutional union of the UK needs a radical overhaul – a slavish embrace of old unreformed Unionism doesn't make sense.
- Recognises the models of the Nordic countries and other western democracies, regardless of our destination as a nation, and talks up a new vision for social partnership, health, education, employment and public services.
- Stops rejecting another Independence referendum. It is going to happen sometime. There is no point arguing against democracy and there could be a second question next time: federalism.
- Believes that patriotism is modern, attractive, and less divisive than nationalism. Whether you are Scottish or British or

European, people can also be patriots of Humanity. Labour must start to use this language against the SNP and the Tories. Identity is okay.

- Thinks a written constitution for Britain and Scotland is long overdue. Acknowledging the fact that Westminster may be uninterested, Labour and other parties in Scotland should proceed on its own.
- Needs to talk more about the economy and progressive taxation in light of the new Social Security and taxation measures recently devolved. Regardless of Scotland's constitutional destination, a sound economy is vital to every aspect of life.
- Believes that human rights, employee rights and the role of Trade Unions are as important today as they were in 1900; social partnership on the German and European models is the way forward. These workplace issues should be protected in any constitutional framework.

Scotland needs to be driven forward with new and powerful ideas.

Breaking free from the past, retaining timeless principles and a history that fired Labour in 1900 and establishing, unlike other parties in Scotland, a serious and sustainable assault on inequality is the way forward; this is what will determine credibility, relevance and, respect.

A consensus has to be built around a positive case for Scotland's role within a modern and transformed Union. There was a consensus in 1997 devolution, but today the nation is divided with both campaigns making this worse. We need a cohesive nation-building campaign.

Scottish political parties must campaign for a new written constitution for the UK which, at its core, abandons the idea of the absolute sovereignty of the Westminster Parliament. This has become redundant as a consequence of the ECHR, the EU and devolution. In the early days of his Premiership, Gordon Brown talked about building the trust of the British people in our democracy, and argued for, 'a shared national consensus for a programme of constitutional reform'. This chimes with today's reality where we need to peer into the future, look closely at the current constitutional set up and, within that, the needs of Scotland. Without this wider perspective of reform, the case for the Union is weakened and the prospect of further political instability is increased. This is the point of engagement for the Unionist parties at Westminster, especially Labour who have much to gain from a solution which satisfies the settled will of the Scottish people and makes long term sense for the Union. The longer Scotland is out there on its own, the greater the danger that it will eventually have no other option that separation. The importance of this cannot be overstated.

We need a vision of Scotland that is positive, radical and transformational, and at the same time we need to tell Scots, disillusioned by austerity and Tory policies at Westminster, that the Union has a new story to tell. The mere fact that the Union has existed for 306 years is no guarantee of its continued relevance or popularity. The world is changing and so are the generations.

Although largely often unnoticed, the impact of the corrosive and toxic policies of the Tories at Westminster is widening the political divide between Scotland and the Union and making the era of Thatcherism look benign in comparison.

New political realities are opening up. The volatility of voters, the unstable nature of the UK, the deepening inequality in Scotland, no clear decision on the Scotland question, and the short term nature of our politics provide the backdrop for a way back. The constant drip feed of more powers is neither a strategy nor a long term solution. Trying to be more left than the SNP – whose credentials are suspect anyway – makes little sense. Trying to fight nationalism with more nationalism, makes even less sense. Trying to fight populism with more populism is wrong.

Labour has, within its own rich history, achievements, internationalism, social progress, philosophy, principles and core values: all it needs to once again be a successful party. But it has to dig deep and rediscover them. It needs to win the battle of ideas and have a narrative or story for Scotland which resonates with the public, a story that is compelling, relevant and credible and delivered with confidence and self-belief.

Labour in Scotland should aim to be the voice of Scotland and lead the debate for a radical shake up of the wider constitutional framework of the UK.

Above the noise there is a confident nation trying to be heard, trying to assert itself and trying to move ahead at a time of great uncertainty in Scotland, the UK in Europe and world-wide. Rebuilding trust is the key to winning back the political affection of a nation that has simply drifted away from Labour, often more in sorrow than in anger.

This is the new normal. Labour has to be bold about its intentions, passionate about its actions and reconnect with the electors.

England, masquerading as Britain, and exhibiting the worst excesses of extreme Conservatism and narrow nationalism, is the threat to the Union. So if England is the problem, what is the solution? Are Scots, divided 50/50 on the Independence question, still looking for a way to stay in the Union, or is that alternative fast receding?

Federalism could help answer both questions, but time is running out. Federalism is complex, has many forms, requires leadership and vision, and is a tough constitutional alternative. Embracing and promoting federalism could provide Scots with a real choice and a positive alternative to Independence. No one should be in any doubt, however, that the path to a federal UK is strewn with political land mines, massive obstacles, constitutional chasms and the history factor where centuries of 'ruling the waves and empire' have created a delusional Westminster, seemingly incapable of change. For the SNP, interdependence in the EU will become the rallying call, out of one Union and into, for them, a much more attractive, more welcoming and more prosperous other Union. No one should underestimate the powerful political message this offers. Brexit has made the future of Britain more complex and confused, but some issues remain crystal clear. Scotland has limited real political or constitutional power in what remains a Britain dominated by the ideas of the absolute sovereignty of the Westminster Parliament, the assumed superiority of that institution, the closed community of London based politics and an increasingly authoritarian mindset dictated by Downing Street – and no written constitution.

The 1997 Scotland White Paper and three Scotland Acts have given Scotland power over certain policies but no significant power over politics, governance and the constitution, where all roads still lead to Westminster. Power devolved is not power shared. If change is to mean anything then the crucial question becomes: What would a federal union look like?

A new debate on federalism would have to face up to Westminster power and authority, the deep seated resistance to changes in the way we are governed, and a mindset shaped by 300 years of political and constitutional history. England, the voice that dominates Westminster and was responsible for Brexit, is also significant part of the problem.

Federalism can offer an alternative to Independence, but it has to be based on a total reshaping of political and constitutional power and authority within the UK. The devolution of more 'powers' on their own, dressed up as federalism lite, where Westminster is unable or unwilling to loosen its grip on political power, is not federalism.

The idea of a federal union has been around for some time. Winston Churchill was a visionary, whose speeches on Europe and Scotland in the early part of the 20th century were remarkable prescient. His Zurich speech in 1946, predating the creation of the EU, predicted a 'United States of Europe'. Much earlier in his life, in a speech to his Dundee constituency on 9 October 1913, he said,

> Another great reason for the settlement of the Irish question in the present Parliament... is that the ground is thereby cleared for the consideration of claims of self-government for other parts of the United kingdom besides Ireland. You will remember how, last year, I addressed a meeting in Dundee on this subject. I made it clear that I was not speaking of the immediate future, but dealing with the subject which lay for the moment outside the sphere of practical politics and raising a question for reflection and discussion rather than for prompt action.
>
> I spoke of the establishment of a federal system in the UK, in which Scotland, Ireland and Wales, and, if necessary, parts of England, could have separate legislative and parliamentary institutions, enabling them to develop, in their own way, their own life according to their own ideas and needs in the same way as the great and prosperous States of the American Union and the German empire.

This was a remarkable speech.

There is no fixed model of federalism. It is best defined as two levels of government, each of which has independent powers and neither has supreme authority over the other. Devolution doesn't meet the criteria. This is why we have to be very careful about selling 'devo plus' or 'devo unionism' as federalism. The best known and most studied example is the US. Setting aside the size of England, there are a number of problems facing a push for federalism. What are the distinguishing characteristics of federalism, the major political issues to be tackled and the important tests that have to be passed?

First, it requires a written and accessible constitution, something the UK doesn't have. Federations in Germany, Canada and the US have strong constitutions. In the case of a federation the national constitution distributes the constitutional powers of government between the two levels. Neither level of government in a federation receives its power from the other. They do not receive their respective powers from legislation enacted by the national legislature. They come from a common source, the national constitution. So in operation, Scotland would not be completely or virtually independent. It would, though, possess a substantial degree of autonomy and self-government.

Second, England would require a constitutional status similar to the other nations of the UK, and in this context it would have a Parliament or Assembly that is not Westminster. The voice of England at Westminster continues to drown out the other nations.

Third, the House of Lords would be abolished in its current form and instead could host representation from each of the nations –and possibly regions – of the Union. This would breathe new life into a second chamber, reflecting people and politics, not privilege, the establishment or the elite.

Fourth, the absolute sovereignty of Westminster – a doubtful reality anyway – would end. The new constitution would set out the terms of this new political settlement and act as a check on Westminster's powers and confirmation that federalism was, for the first time, giving power to people and their nations. Devolution gives away or devolves some of its authority where, as under federalism the separation of power is permanent and enshrined in a separate constitution. Powers must transfer from Westminster to the people.

Fifth, reform of the electoral system and the scrapping of the discredited first-past-the-post system would boost democracy and provide a fairer representation of the votes and the values of our diverse Union and curb political extremes and excesses.

Sixth, more areas of policy – including immigration, welfare and employment – would fall to the four nations or be shared. There would be a recasting of the institutional structure of the Union and, like other European countries, certain European and international matters could be agreed through dialogue and joint and binding decision making.

Seventh, the arguments for, and the delivery, of this far reaching alternative would embrace the idea that federalism is about sharing power and cannot be sold as tinkering with UK governance and sovereignty. This would be a deception.

Eighth, a fairer distribution of political and constitutional power in the UK would help strengthen our increasingly fragile democracy.

Ninth and finally, setting aside the distinctive features of a federal union and the constitutional and political changes this would require, how is all of this to happen? A Constitutional Convention would be an important first step. Wales, Scotland and Northern Ireland could lead, but England has to be part of the solution and currently remains detached from mainstream 'four nation' thinking.

This is a tough agenda. Failure to move on some or all of these far reaching reforms could reinforce the view that the politics of Scotland and the rest of the UK are diverging and irreconcilable. The rejection of federalism could mean the last throw of the Westminster dice leading inevitably to a UK that seems to have run out of political options.

Are there any prospects of Westminster and the traditional parties, being able to offer, deliver and share real power with any of the nations of Britain? This is were modernity could meet the brick wall of history and exceptionalism.

As polls continue to show a divided Scotland, have Scots reached a point where federalism could be a way forward?

Federalism deserves a serious airing. Theresa May talks about 'strengthening the ties between nations' in the UK, while smashing our ties with the EU, and ignoring the pleas of Northern Ireland and Scotland over Brexit. Labour should be less concerned with the timing of a second Independence referendum and instead put all their efforts into a federal alternative as the way forward and as the possible basis of a second question on the next ballot paper, whenever it happens. The status quo is not an option for Scotland's future. The Tories can't be trusted with either the future of Britain or Scotland. The PM's 'Britain Alone' future – and her delusional comments about 'Brexit making the UK stronger' – threaten all of us.

Using Churchill's insight, questions remain. Is federalism now inside the 'sphere of practical politics', or is it just about 'reflection and discussion rather than for prompt action', or are we speaking 'of the immediate future', or just dreaming of a new political order that can never be?

This would be end the absolute sovereignty of Westminster. The new constitution would be a check on Westminster's powers and confirmation that federalism was, for the first time, giving power to people and their nations. This is a vital part of giving power to the citizen.

Federations come in many forms. Adopting a federal solution makes sense for the Labour party. The advocacy of this far reaching alternative must accept that this is not devo plus. Federalism is about power and cannot be sold as tinkering with UK governance and sovereignty. This would be a deception.

For many, federalism will mean no more than devolution, so a reasonably simple matter then of changing the language, but not the substance. For others who want a radical alternative, there will be political mountains to climb. This begs the questions of whether it is too late, too little or too impossible.

Brexit isn't going to work and this could be the spark that once again ignites the flames of unrest and leads more Scots to think that Britain under the Tories and out of the EU is a poor deal.

It is only Scottish Labour that can create a new debate on federalism and engage the whole country, asking the questions that are central to Scotland's future. The debate needs to move on and widen its scope. Five big questions, which will help Scotland decide, need to be posed by the party and answered by the people:

- Will the gloom and uncertainty about the prospects of a change of Government at Westminster in the next 10–15 years worry Labour voters in Scotland – the most important body of voters still to be won round to radical change – that there is no immediate escape from Tory rule?
- Could the Labour party convince electors that it is capable of delivering federalism as an alternative to independence, but not just as a make-over of the status quo?
- Are there any prospects of Westminster, so steeped in the history of absolute sovereignty, political exceptionalism and collective centralism and now in the grip of English nationalism and authoritarianism, able to offer and share real power with any of the nations of Britain?
- Will Scotland's future ultimately be determined by England's block on Britain's progress, its new and virulent strain of right wing populism and the fact that politically Scotland is diverging so dramatically from England?
- Have Scots reached a point where they have an idea of what Scotland could be, of what kind of society they want to live in, of what vision they have for Scotland in the world and could federalism be a way forward?

It is worth noting that Brexit and the Leave campaign have been rightly criticised for offering no alternative future for Britain on leaving the EU. If Scots decide to leave the UK, that mistake can't be repeated: federalism is an alternative.

These are questions for people who don't support Scottish nationalism, the SNP or Independence and haven't been interested in or supportive of radical change. This is the 50 per cent who remain unconvinced and uninspired by the current debate. In the current chaos of a declining UK and the madness of Brexit, they could be sympathetic to the idea of a different future for their country.

Brexit has made the debate about Scotland's future more confused, complex and uncertain. The timeline is hard to define. The battle lines and big issues remain clear. The federalist option deserves a serious airing.

Next time round, excluding some unforeseen intervention, Scotland will have to decide between two different futures: either being in the EU or in the UK. Black Friday confirmed we cannot have both. This is the choice that Scots will have to make. The idea of Independence is firmly rooted in the minds of many Scots. This will not change unless there is an alternative that makes practical sense and captures their ideals and imagination.

Brexit, however, means Scotland out of the EU. Winning the EU back for Britain and then achieving federalism within Britain, may be the solution that prevents a lifetime of 'neverendum' and the constitutional question hoovering up all our political energies for decades to come.

On the other hand, there are huge question marks about whether Westminster and the political classes have either the interest or the vision to deliver this. This solution requires the whole of the UK to undertake a never attempted reconstruction of the nation state and a sharing of real power with its four nations. This idea is not even on the radar scheme of Westminster, never mind the drawing board! The condition of England and its politics, is of deep concern. Any lingering sense of Britishness, on my part is slowly ebbing away.

Westminster is simply failing Scotland and Scots who want to remain in the UK. The collapse of England and its politics and the lack of any long term thinking at Westminster on constitutional matters are driving Scotland towards Independence. Britain – more accurately England – is the problem, but what is the solution? England voted to leave and is now moving away from Scotland. A hard Brexit could have disastrous consequences for the economy. Abandoning the 'free movement of people' and leaving both the Single Market and the Customs Union will not be in Scotland's interests. This is not the deal that was on offer to Scots in September 2014, and represents a destruction of the spirit of the Union and the removal of any pretence that real constitutional power was being devolved to Scotland in the Scotland White paper delivered 20 years ago. The Tories are changing the rules of Scotland's membership of the UK and undermining the reasons for being a member, and no one is being consulted.

To be independent in the full constitutional, 'sovereign', and political sense requires a much greater degree of consensus and a deeper understanding of the likely consequences. Scots have to convince that they are clear about what is best for Scotland. The traditionalists, the fundamentalists and those who argue for Scotland to be independent at any price, need no further persuasion, but the majority of Scots – passionate, patriotic but pragmatic – still remain unconvinced. This is where a better case has to be made

The PM's actions so far – no to an early independence referendum, the rejection of any serious role for Scotland in the EU negotiations, the promotion of the voice of England through Westminster, and the deafening silence to any mention of a four nation union – suggest an uphill struggle to advance the case for constitutional change. Scotland's role looks marginal, as Theresa May focuses on securing Britain's exit from the EU. The prospects of another five years of Tory rule at Westminster will also concentrate the minds of Labour voters in Scotland; out of the EU, with little prospect of a federal solution and no immediate prospects of a Labour government at Westminster, may force more Scots to think of new ideas and a different future.

The Prime Minister's conversion to a snap election on 8 June 2017, may have been caused by panic – more necessity than choice. Maybe she couldn't risk waiting until the Article 50 negotiations were complete because of the 2020 elections and a contest being fought on a disastrous set of outcomes. Maybe the EU negotiators are already gaining the upper hand over her inexperienced, ideologically motivated and inept negotiating team. Maybe she is going to be forced to pay a large sum of money in EU compensation, accept the interim authority of the European Court of Justice and live with a limited free movement of people. Maybe she doesn't want the electors to know that the negotiations are not going well and that there will be no parallel talks on trade. Trade will have to wait for years. Maybe the constitutional vote in Turkey showed the folly of celebrating a tiny majority of votes as an overwhelming victory for one side or another. Maybe the support for remaining will grow, buyer's remorse will set in and the noise of Regrexit will get louder. Maybe, as a fledgling autocrat, she wanted to avoid the possibility of Parliament having a decisive vote on the Article 50 outcomes, knowing this will have become a popular idea.

Based on the logic of this growing list of imponderables, Theresa May cut and run. As an authoritarian, she is dismissive of democracy and accountability. She was seeking a one-party Brexit state before her false promises and lies caught up with her and, for the first time, a British election was fought exclusively in England but with potentially dire consequences for Scotland and Northern Ireland. Britain should vote on: her reaction to the insanity of a hard Brexit; the economic nationalism she is keen to pursue; her fetish for Britain resurrecting the idea of the old Atlantic alliance and becoming, at least in concept, the 51st state of the US. A number of issues emerge from this.

If Theresa May pushes for a 'hard Brexit', coming out of the Single Market and pandering to the zealots demanding an end to the free movement of people, many Scots will think the UK Government has taken leave of its senses and face a choice between the UK or the EU. This was not the choice in 2014.

The state of England's politics is challenging and threatens the very fabric of society where any notions of stability, security and solidarity are being trashed by a lurch to the right, and where intolerance and nationalism are creating a bitterly divided Britain.

Theresa May's ill-informed remarks about no four nation veto, no new referendum after negotiations and no serious scrutiny or parliamentary votes on the repeal of the European Communities Act 1972, or the commencement of Article 50, invoke the spirit of an elected dictatorship at Westminster and a serious contempt for democracy. So why should we trust the PM to achieve outcomes that are remotely in the national interest, never mind Scotland's interests?

Our internationalism is being shredded. Scots have a different world view and we are more inclined to embrace a broader and more informed humanity, where the idea of global citizenship, tolerance and compassion are forces for good and the complete antithesis of the intolerance and xenophobia of the cheap patriots. For Scots, not in our name will become a recurrent theme.

Will Westminster ever abandon the absurd idea of absolute sovereignty in a world of shared aspiration and sovereignty? Wallonia, part of Belgium, has a say on an EU trade treaty with Canada, but Westminster will not extend any real power to Scotland.

A consensus or settled will of the Scottish people must emerge. Political parties should unite around the concentration of power and contest the political, legal and constitutional authority of Westminster. There should be an opportunity for the Scottish Government, Parliament and the electors to debate and vote on the outcome of the Brexit negotiations; we should constantly remind Theresa May of our intent.

The traditionalists, the fundamentalists and those who argue for Scotland to be independent at any price need no further persuasion, but most Scots remain unconvinced: this is where a better case must be made and not just about Independence. Slim majorities, as Brexit has shown, can undermine national solidarity and create a bitter legacy that can be enduringly destructive. When does a majority become large enough to justify major constitutional change? When is a matter settled beyond reasonable doubt? Brexit may be influencing hearts and minds in ways that were never envisaged when Scotland voted to remain. The settled will of Scots remains elusive.

What is the point of a union that is unwilling to take Scotland, Wales and Northern Ireland seriously? Interdependence in Europe is a much bigger idea. The diverging politics of Scotland and England may ultimately decide Scotland's destiny.

Sir Walter Scott's words ring true: 'Oh, what a tangled web we weave when first we practise to deceive'. After a campaign of deception, Britain is losing sight of what the truth is. The PM's tactics became a high-risk strategy. This is where hard Brexit could become a nightmare for the PM.

The election, however, has convinced both sides that an early referendum is in neither of their interests. Nicola Sturgeon is holding off a second Independence referendum to try and take part in Brexit negotiations, but if Scotland isn't listened to, a referendum could become a viable option.

Margaret Thatcher shaped Scotland's negative view of Conservatism for nearly a generation, and still does. A few Tory seats gained north of the border may change that mindset, but if May misinterprets what is going on in the flush of an English-based victory, she could accelerate the break-up of the Union.

Brexit has made the debate about Scotland's future more confused, complex and uncertain, but although the timeline is hard to define, the battle lines and big issues remain clear. Let us promote the politics of principle and protest. Let us spend more time ridiculing the populist justifications of Trump and Brexit and denying credence, oxygen and respect to their ideas. Let us put peoples' interests first. Scots have yet to be convinced of the wisdom of independence from the UK i.e. a positive case in addition to reacting to the decline of the Union and the increasingly right wing nature of English politics. Progressivism, patriotism and identity may still trump nationalism.

The constitutional question shouldn't be the sole preserve of the SNP or nationalism; the kind of country we want is the concern of everyone. Brexit may yet be the spark that once again ignites the flames of unrest and leads more Scots to think that Britain under the Tories and out of the EU is a poor deal. The Scottish debate needs to move on and widen its scope.

10

The Way Ahead

WE SHOULD BE having a debate on a new world view built on membership of the EU as a source of prosperity, peace, solidarity and security. These are the benefits of British membership of the EU which isolationists, economic nationalists and the deluded right of British politics can't stomach. Instead, the Government wants us to build on our relationship with the US and pretend that leaving the EU is our salvation. Europe is our future. The challenges and opportunities of continental Europe have everything to do with us. The spectacle of the Conservative party tearing itself apart over Europe only serves to illustrate how far Britain, and in particular the right wing of the Conservative party, has lost its way in world affairs and political honesty.

This is an opportunity for Britain to re-order international and domestic priorities where we work with our European neighbours. This is about sharing sovereignty and ambition. We need to get over much of our history and have a new sense of identity and purpose in this new century.

It's also time for the Labour party to move on. The political alliance of party membership, parliamentary Labour party and the people, must be reconstructed and respected. Abraham Lincoln, in a speech in June, 1858, said, 'A house divided against itself cannot stand'.

But there is more to be done. This requires a public philosophy to compete and contest the market philosophy of the Tories. A series of unifying political themes that in tough times can hold the party together; a political creed, without which people remain confused and mistrustful of what we stand for. An embrace of not only policies but the action required to achieve them, commitment to the equal worth of everyone which combines aspiration and equality and puts citizens before consumers.

The UK needs federalism, but time is running out. Federalism is complex, has many forms, requires leadership and vision and is a tough constitutional alternative. Embracing and promoting federalism could provide Scots with a real choice and a positive alternative to Independence. No one should be in any doubt however that the path to a federal UK is strewn with political land mines, massive obstacles, and constitutional inertia. The history factor, centuries of 'ruling the waves' and empire have created a delusional Westminster, which resists change. For the SNP, interdependence in the EU will become the rallying call out of one Union but into, for them, a much more attractive, more welcoming and more prosperous other Union.

A new written constitution would be a check on Westminster's powers and confirmation that federalism was, for the first time giving, power to people and their nations and taking it away from Westminster.

A new debate is needed. Parties must reach out to the whole country.

A different approach to Brexit is needed. A binding vote in Parliament at the outcome of the negotiations and/or possibly a referendum or the inclusion of commitment to Remain in the manifestos of progressive parties are all possible outcomes. Defeating the EU legislation in the House of Commons over the net two years is another option. From now on, there must be a campaign in the country to highlight the dangers of Brexit. In politics you must stand for something. Brexit is a sell-out of Britain's interests and a life changing catastrophe for the country. In this, the people must take the lead and head for a day of reckoning with the cheap patriots of the Conservative right who are trying to dismantle Britain and impose further austerity and a market run society.

The public has never been more distrustful, disconnected and disillusioned with democracy and governance. Trust between people and politicians has broken down. A quiet revolution simmers. Long term outcomes are unclear and uncertain. A great deal of bewilderment, fragility and anger has settled on our politics, democracy and governance. The word citizen is fast disappearing as market speak further entangles areas of public and social interest far removed from economic interests. The citizen must now become the most important building block in transforming our politics.

In this rapidly changing world there will be far reaching

consequences for how we organise our lives and shape our politics, democracy and governance. Certainties that we have taken for granted are being demolished. While, in the eyes of some, this recalibration was long overdue, for others there are now stark and unsettling choices to be made about how we want to live in the 21st century and what kind of society we want to build.

We are approaching the point where British people need to be protected from the excesses of governments between elections. With no consent other than a mention in a manifesto, a referendum on the EU is pushed through the House of Commons; the public interest plays second fiddle to the interest of the party.

We are fast becoming political subjects, engaged in elections but excluded from ongoing involvement because there is no constitution to reflect the importance of the public will and the important role the citizen has to play in a modern society. The Conservatives want subjects and consumers, but Britain needs citizens.

A new constitution would safeguard our membership of the EU by creating a proper constitutional court, as in Germany and the US, and put the jurisdiction of the European Court of Human Rights and the protections of the European Convention on Human Rights beyond the reach of partisan politics.

We need an informed electorate and progressive politics that reflect change; a Labour party that has a philosophy and effectively exposes the Right in British politics; a party that has a vision for the world we live in and a serious view on how we can be a positive part of change; a party that understands and respects its citizens. We need a party that sees the moral limits and excesses of markets; a party that can articulate the benefits of Government intervention. Above all else, we need a party that both understands and promotes the common good, where an equal society is built around the idea of the equal worth of every child, young person and adult in our country. Tackling inequality must be the major objective.

Scotland has choices in the current political upheaval. Why shouldn't we be like Scandinavia or Germany or other parts of Europe? We are global and European. We have arguments from the right about merely being British, isolated and disconnected from a world, and a Europe, that needs to be more integrated, united and equal. At every turn, right wing politics is in danger of isolating Britain. This is the enemy within. Brexit is an example of the right running amok, on permanent license from weak and spineless Conservative party leadership, who sometimes act as recklessly as those within their party causing most harm. An offer of the past, from the past by the past. There are victories to be won, but progressive politics can't seem to see the opportunities presented to them.

The level of political or public literacy and civic awareness is dangerously low. This allows the right leaning press to promote a party like the Conservatives who are doing enormous damage to Britain.

The UK is not alone in facing these challenges. Throughout Europe and the US, profound social, economic, demographic and technological changes are taking place, holding out the prospect of consequences for our politics, constitutional structures, democracies and governance. For some, this offers an overdue shake up of our remote political process. For others, however, there are concerns about a retreat into a darker place where respect for tolerance, difference, inclusion, internationalism and multiculturalism, is replaced by authoritarianism, isolationism and a trickle-down form of racism and nationalism.

A new battle of ideas is certainly underway but with little consensus as to where this might end up. Regardless of the consequences and outcomes, which will vary by country and continent, the role of people as 'citizens' will undoubtedly be boosted and emerge as the key to understanding what is taking place and then to build a different kind of politics and society. The political landscape is complex.

Understanding the meaning and significance of change – separating the signals from the noise – is a vital part of this reawakening.

This is a vast agenda with a bewildering array of challenges, opportunities and problems to address.

The scale of change, in our politics and society, is breathtaking: Brexit 2016 for Britain and Scotland; the new era, post-2008 global crash, globalisation and neoliberal austerity; the politics of anger, the decline of leadership and a divided Britain; the rise of populism, nationalism and nativism; disillusionment with the politics and parties and the disintegration of traditional loyalties and allegiances; the idea that something is profoundly wrong with the way we live today as the market closes in on every aspect of society and capitalism remains far from managed; a disunited kingdom where sharp differences of race, ethnicity, religion and geography, a 'them and us', are undermining national cohesion, stability and solidarity in Britain; people, in a deeper, spiritual and more philosophical sense, searching for more meaning in their lives, increasingly dominated by materialism, money and the excesses of the market; the distribution of wealth, income and opportunity creating grotesque levels of inequality and injustice; national identity and xenophobia (especially in England) replacing social class and economic solidarity as the drivers of political change and instability; computers, technology and social media redefining our ideas of community and relationships and revolutionising protest, social action and political organisation in ways barely imagined just a few years ago.

People around the world have become disillusioned with traditional politics, disconnected from democratic institutions and despairing of the ability of political parties to tackle and solve their concerns. The stuttering arrival of 'four nation' politics in the UK, the stirring of England, the rise of national identity as an important political influence and the decision to leave the EU are destined to shake up the constitutional structure of the UK.

We need to radically reshape our thinking and ideas. There is an exciting agenda to be tackled:

On politics, by defending its importance in terms of its relevance to the modern age, what needs to be done to strengthen and enhance, and to counter the growing disillusionment of people with their politicians and political parties.

On democracy (from the Greeks, power of the people), why it matters and what needs to be done to resist the intrusion of market principles and thinking into public policy, and to counter, forces that seek to undermine the whole basis upon which we make decisions in the public interest, to help create, at every level of democratic engagement a more informed public and a modern electoral system.

On our constitutional set up in the UK, where a lack of a written, codified and accessible constitution allows Westminster and politicians to take major decisions based on narrow political considerations rather than in the public interest and where the sovereignty of the people and the national interest should be the priorities; the House of Commons is an 'elected dictatorship'. The recent EU Referendum was conceived and executed by the

Prime Minister without any reference to any other body of opinion or knowledge, appropriate safeguards or whether in the circumstances this was the appropriate or the right thing to do. The sovereignty of Westminster is fundamentally undemocratic and at odds with the idea of a modern constitution.

On governance, where outdated practices, archaic procedures and declining public support are the result of institutions, such as Westminster, being prisoners of history, suffocated by inertia and destined by arrogance and elitism to resist change and share sovereignty. Brexit has exposed the lack of leadership in the aftermath of the result.

On what is next for the UK after the decision to leave the EU, and the prospects of Scotland once again revisiting the idea of leaving the UK (Scexit) and the Scottish Government contemplating a second independence referendum leading to independence or 'interdependence in Europe'.

On what a vision for an Independent Scotland could look like. Can there ever be a significant and decisive majority for terminating our membership of the UK, or can a thin majority suffice in taking such a major constitutional step or is a much bigger effort needed to widen the debate and win over more converts? If so, what needs to be done to argue a more credible case for those who are not 'independence at any price' or 'be a nation again' nationalists? There are huge issues to be discussed. What models can we look at? What is the experience of other small nations in Eastern Europe and the Nordic countries within the EU? How long can we go on discussing Scotland's constitutional future?

On an alternative way forward for Scotland. Only one solution will satisfy the SNP but are there other options that could satisfy other parties and command a majority of the people? Or, is this constitutional war of attrition going to exhaust voter interest and prevent political energies being focussed on more immediate issues and policies of concern to the public. Federalism is an idea whose time has come.

On a reinvented Labour party, leading a progressive alternative to the Conservative party and establishing a wider coalition of interest that puts citizens at the heart of a new politics.

On the growing divergence of Scottish and English politics, the widening chasm of understanding of the different political and constitutional issues now dividing the Union and leading to profound splits in public opinion.

On whether the UK, Westminster and the British Conservatives and Labour parties, could ever break free from institutional inertia and democratic centralism to conceive and ultimately deliver an alternative constitutional settlement, federalism, for an old Union which could offer a viable, attractive and sustainable four nation alternative to Independence and which concedes real sovereignty and power.

On the possibility that the Brexit result may never be implemented as the lies and dishonesty of cheap patriots are exposed and the scale of the consequences of leaving the EU are better understood.

On the challenging idea of the citizen to change our political culture.

At its core, *Citizens United* acknowledges and prioritises the importance of people as citizens. The powerful idea of the citizen remains the driving force behind the goals of creating more fulfilling lives for people, building better societies and tackling a growing agenda of global and local problems, issues and opportunities. The meaning, use and significance of the word citizen has largely been lost. It has been buried under an avalanche of labels – consumers, customers, sellers, buyers and investors – to describe people in their various roles in a society now dominated by market considerations. Citizenship is a more noble idea than the more market driven descriptions that are now given to people. It is about people as human beings. Monarchy required people as subjects, markets want consumers, but democracy demands citizens.

We need to build a new concept of *citizen* to give meaning to the ideas of political engagement and democratic involvement. The second volume of this book will look in detail at how this can be achieved in a Britain of unparalleled opportunity, but, as a result of history and decisions like Brexit, going backwards instead of moving confidently forward.

Citizens need to reclaim a role in determining their own destiny and happiness; a society in which citizens participate as equals in transforming their own lives, in a democracy where the odds are not stacked against them and the political system is not rigged to their continuing disadvantage.

References

Barnett, Anthony, 'The Revolt of the Natives: Britain after Brexit', https://www.opendemocracy.net/uk/anthony-barnett/revolt-of-natives-britain-after-brexit

Boyle, Nicholas, 'The Problem with the English: England doesn't want to be just another member of a Team', *The New European*, http://www.theneweuropean.co.uk/top-stories/the-problem-with-the-english-england-doesn-t-want-to-be-just-another-member-of-a-team-1-4851882

Brown, Tom, and McLeish, Henry, *Scotland: The Road Divides* (Luath Press, 2007)

Disraeli, Benjamin, *Sybil: Or the Two Nations* (Oxford University Press reprint, 2017)

Frank, Thomas, *What's the Matter with Kansas? How Conservatives Won the Heart of America* (Henry Holt and Company, 2004)

Jack, Ian, 'With its attic full of national icons, England can't move on. Scotland can', *The Guardian*, https://www.theguardian.com/commentisfree/2017/mar/25/national-england-cant-move-on-scotland-can

Klein, Naomi, *No is Not Enough: Defeating the New Shock Politics* (Allen Lane, 2017)

Major, John, *John Major: The Autobiography* (HarperCollins, 2010)

McCormick, John, *Why Europe Matters: The Case for the European Union* (Palgrave MacMillan, 2013)

Mishra, Pankaj, 'Welcome to the Age of Anger', *The Guardian*, guardian.com/politics//dec/08/welcome-age-anger-brexit-trump

Sandel, Michael, 'A New Politics of the Common Good', in 'A New Citizenship: Reith Lecture', 2009 http://www.bbc.co.uk/programmes/b00kt7rg

Some other books published by **Luath Press**

Trident and international Law: Scotland's Obligations

Edited by Rebecca Johnson and Angie Zelter

ISBN: 978-1-906817-24-4 PBK £12.99

World in Chains – the impact of nuclear weapons and militarisation from a UK perspective

Angie Zelter

ISBN 978-1-910021-03-3 PBK £12.99

As a further generation of nuclear-armed submarines is developed, *Trident and International Law* challenges the legality of UK nuclear policy, and asks who is really accountable for Coulport and Faslane.

Although controlled by the Westminster Government, and to some extent by the US, all of the UK's nuclear weapons are based in Scotland. The Scottish Government therefore has responsibilities under domestic and international law relating to the deployment of nuclear weapons in Scotland.

Public concern over these responsibilities led to the Acronym Institute for Disarmament Diplomacy, the Edinburgh Peace and Justice Centre and Trident Ploughshares organising an international conference, 'Trident and International Law: Scotland's Obligations'. This book presents the major documents and papers, with additional arguments from renowned legal scholars.

Gross violations of international obligations are not excluded from the purview of the Scottish Parliament.
JUDGE CHRISTOPHER WEERAMANTRY

World in Chains is a collection of essays from well-reputed experts in their field, all of which deliver engaging and analytical critiques of nuclear warfare. They point to the changes needed to re-structure society, so that it is based on compassion, co-operation, love and respect for all. Their words inspire us to resist the growing militarisation and corporatisation of our world.

In the past I have often wondered why obviously unethical or inhumane horrors were able to take place, what people were doing at the time to prevent them or what kind of resistance was happening, how many people knew and tried to stop the genocide, slavery, poverty and pollution... I want those who come after my generation to know that, yes, we do know of the dangers of nuclear war, of climate chaos, of environmental destruction. This book will show you that there were many people working to change the structures that keep our world in chains. ANGIE ZELTER

'The most important book you'll never read.' AL KENNEDY

Scotland, the UK and Brexit

Gerry Hassan & Russell Gunson (eds.)

ISBN 978-1-912147-18-2 PBK £12.99

What kind of society do the citizens of Scotland and the UK aspire to live in, and what political and social union is the best way to nurture this? That is something that rightly concerns and is the responsibility of all of us.

The unexpected outcome of the 2017 UK general election means that the UK Government lacks a clear mandate on Brexit and also that the Scottish Government lacks a clear mandate on holding a second Independence Referendum consequent to the material change in circumstance which will be brought about by Brexit.

In this collection of essays from a wide range of leading political specialists, journalists and academics, Hassan and Gunson have assembled a comprehensive guide to Brexit for the UK as a whole, and its constituent parts.

From fisheries and agriculture to higher education and law, the whys and how of Brexit are challenged from all angles. Particular attention is paid to how Brexit will impact Scotland and the viability of a future independent Scotland.

Britain Rebooted: Why Federalism Would Be Good For the Nations and Regions of the UK

David Torrance

ISBN 978-1-910021-71-2 PBK £7.99

Would federalism work in the UK? Wouldn't England dominate a British federation? How would powers be distributed between federal and home nation level? What about the House of Lords?

This new, post-referendum edition of *Britain Rebooted* is more relevant than ever, given the promises of further devolved powers for the nations and regions of the UK.

'An impressive and useful contribution to the constitutional debate... For those interested in saving the United Kingdom, federalism makes a great deal of sense.' MURDO FRASER, *Think Scotland*

'...breaking the hegemony of Westminster across the islands... An old dream, yes. But still one worth fighting for.' OWEN JONES, *The Independent*

'Torrance is one of Scotland's best political commentators...' MATT QVORTRUP, *The Scotsman*

Details of these and other books published by Luath Press can be found at:
www.luath.co.uk

Luath Press Limited

committed to publishing well written books worth reading

LUATH PRESS takes its name from Robert Burns, whose little collie
Luath (*Gael.*, swift or nimble) tripped up Jean Armour at a wedding
and gave him the chance to speak to the woman who was to be his wife
and the abiding love of his life. Burns called one of the 'Twa Dogs'
Luath after Cuchullin's hunting dog in Ossian's *Fingal*.
Luath Press was established in 1981 in the heart of
Burns country, and is now based a few steps up
the road from Burns' first lodgings on
Edinburgh's Royal Mile. Luath offers you
distinctive writing with a hint of
unexpected pleasures.
Most bookshops in the UK, the US, Canada,
Australia, New Zealand and parts of Europe,
either carry our books in stock or can order them
for you. To order direct from us, please send a £sterling
cheque, postal order, international money order or your
credit card details (number, address of cardholder and
expiry date) to us at the address below. Please add post
and packing as follows: UK – £1.00 per delivery address;
overseas surface mail – £2.50 per delivery address; overseas airmail –
£3.50 for the first book to each delivery address, plus £1.00 for each
additional book by airmail to the same address. If your order is a gift,
we will happily enclose your card or message at no extra charge.

Luath Press Limited
543/2 Castlehill
The Royal Mile
Edinburgh EH1 2ND
Scotland
Telephone: +44 (0)131 225 4326 (24 hours)
Email: sales@luath. co.uk
Website: www. luath.co.uk